What People Are Saying About Fin Tales

"Of the many Detroit automotive executives that made their mark, John Smith was one of the very closest to the center of action—and one of the most articulate. His insights, stories, and analysis will help you understand Cadillac's long history as one of the nation's most illustrious brands."

— Doron Levin, business/finance/automotive journalist for *The Wall Street Journal, New York Times, Detroit Free Press*, and Bloomberg; author of *Irreconcilable Differences: Ross Perot Versus General Motors* and *Behind the Wheel at Chrysler*

"The inside story about the genesis of Cadillac's rebirth—by the ultimate insider."

— Csaba Csere, automotive journalist and former Technical Director and Editor-in-Chief, *Car and Driver*

"*Fin Tales* has taken me back to a time when I thought Cadillac was a goner, but then John took over and we soon had a plan to win. He doesn't take enough credit in this book for all that was accomplished."

— Carl Sewell, Chairman of Sewell Automotive, a privately-owned collection of 18 premium and luxury vehicle brands; author of *Customers for Life: How to Turn That One-Time Buyer Into a Lifetime Customer*

"Into Cadillac's depressing condition of the late '90s stepped John Smith who, along with another 'believer' in the brand's renaissance, Wayne Cherry—who headed up GM's Design Staff—created a new direction under the Art & Science banner, overcame considerable internal opposition, and obtained corporate approval for a massive investment in a series of new models that caused the automotive world to take notice once more."

— Bob Lutz, former Vice Chairman of General Motors and Chrysler, and senior executive positions at BMW and Ford; author of *Guts: Eight Laws of Business from One of the Most Innovative Business Leaders of Our Time*, *Car Guys vs Bean Counters: The Battle for the Soul of American Business*, and *Icons and Idiots: Straight Talk on Leadership*

Fin Tales

Saving Cadillac, America's Luxury Icon

John Smith

AVIVA
PUBLISHING
New York

Fin Tales: Saving Cadillac, America's Luxury Icon

Published by:
Aviva Publishing
Lake Placid, NY (518) 523-1320 www.AvivaPubs.com

Address all inquiries to:
Smithworks LLC
John Smith
4006 Brookside Road
Clarkston, Michigan 48346
313-268-1585
johnsmithjfs@gmail.com
LinkedIn.com/in/johnsmithjfs

ISBN: 978-1-63618-166-0
Library of Congress Control Number: 2021925744

Editors: Larry Alexander and Tyler Tichelaar, Superior Book Productions
Cover Design: Nicole Gabriel, Angel Dog Productions
Interior Book Layout: Nicole Gabriel, Angel Dog Productions
Author Photo: Roland Smith, Last Light Films

All images courtesy of GM Design Archive & Special Collections, General Motors LLC, except Figures 3 and 6.

Every attempt has been made to properly source all quotes.
Printed in the United States of America
First Edition

2 4 6 8 10 12

For Sam and Catherine

ACKNOWLEDGMENTS

I have wanted to share the inside story of Cadillac's turn-around in the late 1990s for some time now. The regrettable COVID-19 pandemic provided the opportunity to finally set it down in black and white.

My time at Cadillac was made possible by Jack Smith, GM's former chairman and CEO. I have always been grateful for Jack's friendship and support during my GM career and happily acknowledge that upfront.

The work at Cadillac was a kind of joint venture with GM's vice president and design director, Wayne Cherry. Wayne and his team were invaluable in getting to Art & Science branding/positioning for Cadillac, which put the brand back on the map in terms of unique and expressive design.

The positioning work was also a labor of love for the Cadillac leadership team—Pete Gerosa, Martin Walsh, Jeff Heichel, Kim Brink, Pat Kemp, Dave Nottoli, Jay Spenchian, Susan Docherty, Ed Berger, Julie Hamp, and Chris

Preuss (Julie and Chris being two of the very best communications pros I have ever worked with!). A very special mention is owed Peter Levin, may he rest in peace, who led the Cadillac work group during this journey. He was a force to be reckoned with!

Thank you to other GM colleagues who, as will be evident in the book, helped the turnaround along, like Rick Wagoner and Ron Zarrella. Ron and I had our differences at times but, when it really mattered, he always showed up.

Many thanks are due to the numerous Cadillac dealers who rallied around Art & Science, some playing important roles on the ground floor—legendary and brand-passionate folks like Carl Sewell, John Bergstrom, John Lund, Joe Serra, Ed Williamson, and many others—for whom, along the way, a GM franchise was probably their family's first retail automotive deal.

For the book itself, thanks go to Jim Boehm, a fraternity brother and GM colleague who helped with unit sales volume and market share data. Thanks as well for the many cold-reads and critiques from the likes of Wayne Cherry,

Bob Lutz, Pete Gerosa, Rico Digirolomo, John Costin, Julie Hamp, and Chris Preuss. I'd also like to thank Doron Levin and David Welch, published authors and veteran auto journalists, for their review of a draft along the way.

A big thank you also to GM's Heritage Center and the GM Design Archive & Special Collections team for allowing me to include various images that illustrate the degree of change that was Art & Science. Few places will instantly bring a smile to your face like the Heritage Center and its collection of decades of great GM cars and trucks! I also want to thank Tom Berthiaume and Parallel Productions for the use of the lovely '60 Eldorado image also included in this book. As will be noted, it was inspirational!

Finally, I give thanks to (and for) my wife Nancy Smith, most especially for her patience. I have talked about writing this book for some time, and the writing and editing of it must have seemed never-ending!

Contents

FOREWORD

By
Robert "Bob" A. Lutz

Large car corporations that own luxury brands tend to husband them poorly. They over-focus on the profitability of the brand's aura, while failing to make the investments necessary to maintain the required exclusivity and desirability. In the terminal phase of a luxury brand's decline, it becomes little more than an ordinary car, sharing platforms and major components with its mass-market corporate cousins. Thus it was with Cadillac, once the symbol of American technological and quality prowess, whose offerings were permitted to evolve into little more than more-or-less differentiated versions of GM's other cars.

Uncompetitive against the newly-arrived luxury brands

like Mercedes and BMW, Cadillac increasingly wound up in that last resort of unwanted new cars: the daily rental fleets. By the late 1990s, the situation seemed irreversibly hopeless.

Into this depressing situation stepped the author. Together with Wayne Cherry, head of GM design and a fellow believer in the Cadillac brand's ability to be restored to glory once again, they obtained corporate approval for the massive capital investment needed to revive the brand. A new design direction, "Art & Science," together with new engines and an infusion of youth-oriented performance models, were part of the plan. Despite considerable internal opposition and copious second-guessing, John Smith, Wayne Cherry, and their teams persisted and produced a series of vehicles, beginning with the CTS, that caused the automotive world to take notice.

The CTS, SRX, and XLR sports roadster were highly acclaimed in the media, while the ultra-high-performance V-Series cars showed that Cadillac could match or better the hallowed German performance sedans. But while sales and margins improved nicely, the old adage that it takes a generation to reverse negative brand beliefs, return to consistently higher volumes, and again dominate the US luxury market proved true. As of this writing, the story of Cadillac is unfinished.

Will the move to full electrification permit the brand to return to world-beating dynamics and performance, in addition to opulence in style and features? Or will it merely be "comparable" to the best? Today, many highly-skilled men and women at GM are committed to Cadillac's future. They are continuing the struggle successfully commenced by the author and his team. I wish them every success.

INTRODUCTION

t was as if a spaceship had dropped into our backyard....

Parked in the driveway, gleaming in the sun, was Aunt Helen's '59 Eldorado convertible: white, red leather interior, top down, twin bullet tail lamps mounted on tail fins almost as tall as me—menacing as machine guns—yards of chrome, and an AM/FM signal-seeking stereo radio. Yikes! She always had a new Cadillac, but this baby...well, it spoke to me in ways only the passage of time would fully reveal.

I was nine years old, and Aunt Helen was my mother's younger sister. She had driven down from Detroit to visit us in Kansas City. I was already drawn to the car business by the occasional visits to Kansas City of Helen's husband, Bill Mosher. He was a tall, athletic, and good-looking "car guy," hair combed back, and always sporting white tab-collared shirts. He was a senior manufacturing exec at Chevy, and he would come to town to check out firsthand how the Chevrolet-Kansas City assembly plant was running. People, including me at that tender age, were drawn to his personality and lifestyle—flying about on the company turboprop, overnighting at the Muehlebach Hotel, and always driving the newest iron! He had a neat job working around cars; what more could any kid aspire to?

Thirty-seven years later, in October 1996, I had dinner in Detroit with Ron Zarrella, who was recruited to General Motors (GM) from Bausch & Lomb for the express purpose of turning GM into a first-class marketing machine. I'd observed Ron's work from a distance since by then I was President of GM's Allison Transmission Division in Indianapolis. He was making a whole lot of changes...basically teaching and installing brand management across all of GM's North American brands—Chevrolet, Pontiac,

Buick, GMC, Oldsmobile, Cadillac, and Saturn. (Hummer was added to the pile in 1998.) Ron did so with the blessing and encouragement of GM's senior leaders, including the Board of Directors, because GM's market share had steadily fallen to around 30 percent by the mid-1990s from its 50 percent peak in 1962.

While it was mostly a get-to-know-you session, it was clear Ron planned to offer me a general manager position, either at Oldsmobile or Cadillac. I was only interested in Cadillac because it represented the best that General Motors could be, and it needed a lot of work to measure up to the so-called "noble marques": Mercedes and BMW. I wanted that challenge, and I thought my four-and-a-half years living and working in Europe gave me a useful closeup on one of the most discriminating luxury vehicle markets in the world.

I got the job, effective February 1, 1997, and this book

chronicles the work during my three years there. A dedicated and passionate team pulled Cadillac back from the brink, reimagined the brand around a new positioning strategy called Art & Science, and executed the plan with creativity and verve.[1]

Before we go further, three truths need be told upfront: first, the car business is big and complicated, consumes huge amounts of resources, and involves contributions from a lot of people—and that's when a brand is running well; second, restoring Cadillac attracted a lot of "interest" within GM, some of it not always helpful which, while distracting, was mostly overcome with passion, patience, and persistence; third, fixing an automobile brand takes time since the first new vehicle that conveys a brand's new (or renewed) values can take four-plus years to bring to market.

---

1 Note: As will be explained later in the book, the Art & Science strategy encompassed: a design language for all Cadillac models (some would say form vocabulary) that visually conveys the brand's values; technology and contenting priorities; a target audience; and supporting distribution and marketing plans.

The rescue of Cadillac wouldn't have occurred without Wayne Cherry, GM's design chief at the time, and the talented, Art & Science-Kool-Aid-drinking Cadillac leadership team, and certainly not without the support…and downfield blocking…provided by Jack Smith, Rick Wagoner, and (when it really mattered) Ron Zarrella.

Cadillac dealers and the Cadillac Dealer Council also played a big role in the turnaround. Given hope, they heaved to and made significant improvements to their facilities and sales processes. Many individual dealers deserve to be thanked, but I will single out Carl Sewell from Dallas for his early and sustained leadership, ideas, and support.

After I departed from Cadillac in 2000, responsibility for leading the turnaround passed from my hands to others, notably Mark LaNeve and Jim Taylor, who were well-supported by the superb crew of GM designers, engineers, and manufacturing folks in the trenches who rose to the occasion. They, too, wanted Cadillac to be great again.

Art & Science saved Cadillac and, through 2005, drove improvements of all the right kinds—sales, market share, profits, and demographics. Sadly, the brand's performance in North America has mostly deteriorated since then, although sales volumes in China have been more than offsetting. While this is good news, depending on China for a decent overall result is not without its complications, most importantly around the brand's positioning and heritage long-term. In any event, it cannot be comforting for Cadillac to be flirting again with irrelevance on its home turf.

There *is* hope for Cadillac because GM's top leaders have placed it at the head of the company's pell-mell, "everybody in" changeover to an all-electric portfolio of cars, trucks, and crossovers. That suggestion was so much wine-before-its-time during my time at Cadillac, but better late than never!

CHAPTER 1

HOPE

n early 1997, Cadillac was in a pretty sad state, having experienced declining sales, market share, and image for nearly twenty years. Unit sales and market share were half of what they were at Cadillac's peak in 1978, despite 50 percent growth in the luxury market. Once the luxury vehicle of choice—the favorite of presidents, movie stars, and industrialists—celebrated in more than 200 songs, and being synonymous with top quality products—the Cadillac of personal watercraft, etc.—Cadillac was looking tired and irrelevant compared to Mercedes, BMW, and even the newbie, Lexus. Car buff books and media observers were writing Cadillac off for dead.

Cadillac dealers had suffered, too, and rated their franchise dead last in NADA's (National Automobile Dealers Association) annual survey of all franchised auto dealers in the US. Dispirited dealers also held back on improving their facilities, with obvious adverse effects on Cadillac's image and sales.

The high-volume Cadillac dealers in urban centers had a less difficult time, and some still managed to provide truly excellent care to their customers despite the lack of a compelling product line. In fact, third-party surveys would show that Cadillac still remained among the top franchises when it came to customer satisfaction and service.

Cadillac's decline was largely self-inflicted, as the market for luxury vehicles was strong and growing—consistent with generally rising incomes in the US. But luxury trends were changing as well, and Cadillac was slow to adapt, sometimes showing signs of the old brilliance but, more often than not, displaying undue caution.

The '92 STS was a dramatic and critically-acclaimed new product, winning the *Motor Trend* Car of the Year award and suggesting the brand was back on track. Unfortunately, two years later, a new Deville was introduced, which many regarded as bloated and over-bodied. And it looked even worse if you added the rear-wheel fender skirts! Perfect for any episode of *The Sopranos*.

Once the embodiment of American ingenuity, optimism, and exuberance, Cadillac designs mostly fell short of their historic daring, long a central part of Cadillac's value. No advertising or customer care could overcome the uninspiring and floaty hardware that Cadillac had become known for.

How Did Cadillac Get Here?

While the brand itself cannot be left off the hook, the answer has more to do with GM than it does with Cadillac.

The *Cliff's Notes* version might start by noting that GM's best-year-ever was 1965—market share of nearly 50 percent, net income margin of 10.3 percent, and a debt-equity ratio of 0.04 (basically debt-free). Fast forward to 1996 and market share was 31 percent, net income margin was 3.2 percent, and the debt-equity ratio was 3.64 (or 5.81 if future pension and healthcare obligations were included). For perspective, anything above 2.0 is considered risky. To put a sharper point on it, net debt in 1996 was more than $70 billion!

What the hell happened?

In the intervening years, GM was confronted by a host of adverse external forces, and its responses obviously fell short. Chief among these forces were antitrust threats, a tsunami of imports in the '60s, the advent of OPEC (Organization of the Petroleum Exporting Countries) bringing permanently higher gas prices, and the first fuel economy regulations in the late '70s, coupled with some truly awful and costly labor agreements along the way.

The antitrust threat was abated, with GM no doubt contributing to this outcome by creating the General Motors Assembly Division (GMAD) in 1968, which took control of all vehicle assembly plants previously managed by the car divisions and Fisher Body. This move would make a mandated spin-off of any one division, like Chevrolet, very difficult and of questionable value to any buyer.

A steady stream of additional consolidations/reorganizations/centralizations followed, with the net effect being threefold: 1) Alfred Sloan's business model featuring empowered and independent car divisions (with some ring-fencing to avoid undue overlap in the market) was replaced with a more centralized and *function*-based organization, e.g., strong engineering, manufacturing, purchasing, and a new, consolidated sales, service and marketing unit; 2) the "car divisions," those closest to the customer, had been reduced to sales and marketing entities, no longer controlled vehicle development, and lost their seats at the big table where strategy and resource allocation decisions are made; and 3) the long-standing *balance* between GM's business and product interests at the very top of the company was lost.

On this latter point, the fully-equipped car divisions were historically a training ground for future company presidents, folks like Ed Cole and Pete Estes. Ed or Pete could hold their own with any company chairman or board on product matters and provided everyday cheerleading and management of the legions of designers, engineers, and marketeers working on the next cool things. When Pete Estes retired in 1981, twenty years would pass until GM would again have such balance at the top of the company. This would be Bob Lutz, whom the company hired as Vice Chairman of Product Development in 2001.

In the meantime, the company paid a high price for product decisions heavily influenced by the engineering and manufacturing leaders and their embrace of "common" solutions. To be fair, there was gold in them thar hills since GM was the largest car company on the planet; the most proliferated when it came to discrete vehicle platforms, engines, transmissions, brakes, radios, screws, etc.; and poorly organized in the sense that there were multiple engineering, manufacturing, and purchasing entities across the globe, most especially in the US. Simply said, more than one global engineering team in any organization is a recipe for redundancy and waste, and GM had more than a handful!

The steady erosion in unit sales, market share, and profits demanded action, and the underlying intent of the many reorganizations and consolidations was, as a totally reasonable endgame, the getting to *one*—one design team, one engineering team, one manufacturing team, one purchasing team, etc.—such that the company could take full advantage of one of its biggest assets, its unmatched size.

This work was taking place at the same time GM was responding to the new fuel economy regulations enacted in 1979. Over the following decade, GM would undertake massive change in its passenger car architectures, moving nearly everything from rear-wheel-drive to the lighter and more fuel-efficient front-wheel-drive (FWD). Engines and transmissions would also necessarily change, meaning nearly every part of every car was changing almost at once. GM did not manage so much change very well, and many of the new FWD vehicles had quality problems. Many of those vehicles were also smaller (and lighter) than the previous models, confounding and confusing customers.

You might think that every car company had the same challenge and GM just cocked it up. Not so. Sure, Ford and

Chrysler had the same regulatory requirements to meet, but their fleets were already somewhat smaller and lighter. The imports, however, had a *lot* less to do because their offerings lined up with the smaller vehicles they already sold in their home markets of Japan and Europe.

Layered on top of this huge fuel-economy-regulation-driven engineering and manufacturing effort was the unique and unaddressed challenge of GM's go-to-market strategy. Despite a near twenty-point loss in market share, in 1997 GM was *still* going to market with the same six brands it had in 1965, plus Saturn, which it added in 1985! No other manufacturer offered any more than three brands, and most offered only one or two.

In 1997, all GM brands, except Saturn, which was new, were scrambling to produce a product line-up that could sustain a dealer network built for different times. Despite attempting to retain its historic multi-brand strategy, the money and design/engineering capacity to carry on with historic and meaningful differentiation just wasn't there, yielding inevitable compromises like the Cadillac Cimmaron, which was no more than a Chevy Cavalier in a tuxedo, and the four not-so-very-different GM mid-sized entries (Chevy, Pontiac, Buick, Oldsmobile) featured on the cover of *Fortune* magazine in August 1983.

Sloan disrupted the nascent automobile market with GM's multi-brand strategy and achieved great success as a result. But the company had been slow to respond to external changes in the market, so "a car for every purse and purpose" became a competitive disadvantage and an unsustainably costly millstone around GM's neck (only remedied by bankruptcy proceedings in 2009 when GM trimmed its lineup down to four brands).

All in all, the '80s were not kind to General Motors. Half of its twenty-point market share loss from its high in 1965 occurred in this decade. With less influence and competing with so many other brand mouths to feed, Cadillac was simply another boxcar on a train that was steadily losing steam.

Beginning to Right the Ship

In 1992, with GM's market share having fallen to below 34 percent and the company edging toward insolvency, the board changed leadership and installed Jack Smith as its new president and CEO. He took many immediate steps to stabilize GM's financial situation, most importantly finding cost savings in purchasing. He also abandoned the venerable GM headquarters building in Detroit and set up shop at the company's technical center in nearby Warren, Michigan. Overnight, GM's monthly committee structure—and its massive underlying ecosystem—disappeared and was replaced with a single, regional strategy

board patterned after GM's successful European operations, which Jack had previously led. Functional leaders
embraced his "common" strategy, and the pursuit of "one"
global company was accelerated by further organizational
consolidation in North America. Getting to one engineering operation, one manufacturing team, one purchasing
team in North America was a necessary prerequisite to
consolidating the four regions' activities into single global
teams. This journey would not be completed until 2005
when *global* product development was created and consolidated under Bob Lutz.

Two actions associated with these changes adversely affected Cadillac. One was GM's focus on revitalizing its
truck offerings. GM did this based on profitability, of
course, but also because the fuel economy standards were
less onerous for this category of vehicles. A lot of money
goes into such vehicles given their many variants (trucks
of varying door configurations, bed lengths, and cargo/

towing capacities; sport utility vehicles of different sizes, etc.) and renovations to the affected assembly plants. In this situation, other vehicles and brands—like Cadillac— just have to wait their turn.

The other action was GM's effort to stabilize and improve market share. John Smale, previously the very successful CEO at Procter & Gamble (P&G), was GM's lead director at the time. He believed GM needed brand management discipline to make its vehicles more appealing, and he had just the fellow in mind to lead the effort—Ron Zarrella from Bausch & Lomb.

Ron joined GM in late 1994 and immediately began leading GM's brand management journey, bringing in experienced brand managers from P&G and other packaged goods companies, while other brand manager candidates were identified from among the high-potential marketing and product cadre within GM. Ron developed clear and repeatable processes, which improved the company's understanding of the customer. That said, Ron decided the "brand" would be the *model* (Silverado) and not the *division* (Chevrolet). This ultimately proved to be unworkable, especially for luxury brands like Cadillac.

Ron also tried to address the "too many mouths to feed" problem through a richly detailed market analysis process called BrandScape. This might be considered *Sloan Redux*, but unfortunately the effort left untouched the *number* of divisional brands the company offered. Absent bankruptcy proceedings, shutting down a car brand in the United States is incredibly expensive because franchised dealers enjoy significant legal protections across the fifty states. (The closure of Oldsmobile in 2000 proved this point, costing GM more than $1 billion!) However, focusing only on where the existing brands best fit left unaddressed GM's growing disadvantage in the market…spreading itself too thin in both product development and marketing…which only got worse when the company acquired Hummer in 1998.

In sum, and paraphrasing from the company's official history, "As GM goes, so goes Cadillac," GM's fortunes had steadily declined and the company was still so much ground under repair in early 1997. Effecting change in a faltering Cadillac brand would no doubt run head-first into swift currents of "common," powerful functional leaders with simplicity uppermost in their minds, the new practice of brand management, and BrandScape-related product portfolio ring-fencing that, on paper, limited opportunities for Cadillac's growth. I could be hopeful that well-reasoned arguments would prevail. Early on, however, this was not my experience, with Ron stating with some energy that "Cadillac is part of GM and its portfolio of brands. It's not BMW or Mercedes, which are stand-alone companies."

That sort of feedback can be off-putting, especially when you are expected to overhaul GM's best brand...from the middle of the organization! (I was three levels removed from GM's chairman.) Had I respected GM's chain of command...had I followed Ron's advice and kept Cadillac in its BrandScape swim lane...it would today be dead and buried.

Back to Hope!

Rick Wagoner was president of GM's North American operations in 1997. By that time, we had known one another for twenty years, having first met playing basketball after business school classes and having worked together initially in GM's New York treasurer's office, later in GM's North American operations, and again at GM Europe from 1989-1992. Tall, affable, and whip smart, Rick rose quickly through GM's financial staff ranks, taking on leadership roles in planning and purchasing along the way to becoming GM's CFO, GM North American president, and ultimately, GM's chairman and CEO.

After I accepted the job at Cadillac, Rick suggested I talk with Carl Sewell, a Cadillac dealer in Dallas. GM was the Sewell family's first car dealership, and Carl had considerably grown the business started by his father. (The Sewell family now operates eighteen stores across the country.) He was, and remains to this day, the only Cadillac dealer who has won Cadillac's Master Dealer designation every year since its inception.

I called Carl soon after arriving at Cadillac. He was easy to talk with, took an interest in my background and early thoughts, and had ideas of his own that he freely shared. Cadillac's decline plainly bothered him practically, but on an emotional level also. Every dealer's business turned on product, or lack thereof, and Carl had no idea where Cadillac was headed as communication between the brand's leadership and its dealers had waned. He was fearful that GM was no longer committed to Cadillac being the best.

Carl knew I would be making the rounds with groups of Cadillac dealers, including those in Texas, to introduce myself and to hear their thoughts and concerns. When I asked him what the most important thing was that I could do for Cadillac dealers during my upcoming visits, Carl simply said, "Give them hope."

While these were my early days at Cadillac, Carl's words rang true. I had just finished a three-year stint managing GM's Allison Transmission Division. Prior to my arrival, Allison had been for sale for two years, but the proposed sale to ZF of Germany was not approved by the US Justice Department. I took charge of a dispirited workforce and distributor community at a business where time had stood still for twenty-four months. Allison was slightly unprofitable, despite commanding 85 percent market share in its core business, which was commercial-duty automatic transmissions. Everybody—customers, employees, distributors, suppliers, and GM—needed confidence in Allison's future. They all needed hope. Over the next three years, we developed and executed a new plan for Allison, significantly growing the business and its profits. Along the way, all the stakeholders were involved, and they found hope, which translated into their commitment to the execution of the new plan.

For Cadillac, its workforce, its loyal if aging owner base, its dealers, and even the automotive media, hope was badly needed. It would take some time to reimagine Cadillac, and there would be friction trying to develop a new vision, let alone navigating any such plan through the GM decision-making process. In the meantime, it was important to listen to all the stakeholders and share my initial thoughts on why a renewed Cadillac was possible and what it might look like.

The first meetings with Cadillac dealers were spirited, and the bell curve was very much in evidence—some were enthusiastic about the possibilities, others were given to unrelenting grousing and complaints, while the rest stood somewhere in the middle. Cadillac's last-place finish on the most recent NADA dealer satisfaction survey was very much in evidence. While I might not have persuaded everyone that their Cadillac businesses would get better soon, they seemed convinced that I'd die trying. Early on, that's all they could ask for.

While on the road meeting dealers, I had already set in motion a top-to-bottom brand review led by Peter Levin from Cadillac, importantly partnering with GM's design staff then led by Wayne Cherry. He was a gifted and passionate designer (with a very dry sense of humor) whom I had worked with at GM Europe in the late '80s and early

'90s. Wayne had lived and worked in Europe for twenty-six years and understood "luxury" and luxury vehicles way better than I did. When I came to Cadillac in early 1997, he was among the first to call. He shared his unvarnished thoughts on the current state of Cadillac design, and offered any and all help his team could provide. He was as annoyed about Cadillac's decline as anyone and noted how his church parking lot in Indianapolis had been repopulated over time, with Mercedes replacing Cadillacs—in the heartland, no less! His contributions to saving Cadillac will be more completely described later, but I have a reason for introducing Wayne now.

In the late spring, early summer of 1997, Cadillac dealers were invited to a meeting in Detroit. Bear in mind that Cadillac had nearly 1,600 dealers in the United States at the time, of which 150 or so were single-point dealers—dealers who sold *only* Cadillacs—and were located in the largest metro areas. Most of these dealers attended, since they accounted for nearly 50 percent of Cadillac sales, but other relatively high-volume Cadillac dealers who also sold other GM models in the same store (GMC and Buick, for example) came as well bringing the total to around 500 dealers. The meeting was held in Detroit's venerable Fox Theatre. Tents with various current and historic Cadillac models were set up in the parking lot across the street.

We were still early in the brand repositioning work and could only speak vaguely about what it might look like, but there were also hopeful points to share with the dealers. The vintage cars on display served as a reminder of Cadillac's rich history and significant accomplishments in both styling *and* technology. We shared third party stories about the lingering reservoir of goodwill for the brand—including excerpts from a Ben Stein article contrasting the soulful driving experience of his Cadillac STS with the drill-press-like character of a Volvo—and also noting the absence of songs extolling the thrill of a road trip in a

Honda!

As a placeholder for our work-in-process ambitions, we got dealers' juices flowing about the better days to come with a full-screen representation of what one of Cadillac's most iconic models, *ever*—the 1959 Eldorado—would look like in 1997 had Cadillac embraced the same attitude-filled design spirit over the intervening years.

That larger-than-life scrim behind me on the Fox stage was worth the trip for many of the visiting dealers, as the collective gasps, hoots, and hollers gave way to sustained applause from the dealer audience. They knew we cared, that we were thinking big, and that we would give it our all.

Their enthusiasm spilled into the parking lot across the street and into the reception preceding dinner. The dealers were upbeat, which was the principal deliverable for this gathering. But while it was the primary topic of discussion, it was not the only thing on dealers' minds.

Since joining Cadillac in February, *every* conversation with dealers included questions about, if not demands for, a luxury truck, as many of their customers (not so much early adopters but certainly fast followers) had been inquiring about when one would be available. And some customers, eager to try something new and different, had already left the fold.

I also believed Cadillac needed an SUV, but at this early point in my tenure, I didn't see a path forward. Brand-Scape expressly limited Cadillac to passenger cars, and every overture I had made to Ron Zarrella had gotten the cold shoulder, and that was on a good day! No doubt, even if he had ever expressed some openness to the idea, the other brand leaders—and his functional peers—could be expected to be quite critical of any deviation from the BrandScape strategy. I listened to the dealers and avoided selling BrandScape, but I also steered clear of making commitments from fear of building expectations that, if not met, would pretty much toss hope into the trash bin.

I resolved to bide my time, feeling sure I would find an opening to revisit the question of a Cadillac SUV, whether by my hand or someone else's.

CHAPTER 2

'SLADE

"It's Mr. Smith."

It was a sunny August afternoon in 1997 when I got the call from Jack Smith, GM's chairman and CEO. I had worked with Jack on several occasions over the preceding twenty years. His full name was John F. Smith, Jr., and our mail had gotten mixed up several times as folks would think his note was from me and vice versa. It was mostly harmless confusion, except for the time payroll slapped his deductions on my gross pay—given his much more senior status in the company, that one hurt!

After some general catching up, Jack asked, "Don't you need a truck?"

I took a deep breath, said yes, and briefly explained why I thought a Cadillac SUV would be good for both the brand and GM. I also said something to the effect that "...but not everyone between me and you would agree."

Jack paused and then said simply, "Let me work on that."

Frankfurt

A few weeks later, I attended the Frankfurt Auto Show, which was probably the most important auto show in the car business at the time. It was held every other year in the sprawling Frankfurt Messe complex. The show included lots of walking between halls, tons of new technology, new models, concept cars and, stashed in remote corners, non-European brands like Cadillac that were seeking exposure and entrée into the large, literate European market. While talking with a journalist, someone told me Jack Smith had just landed, was coming directly to the show, and wanted to see me on the Opel stand.

"Okay, I've asked Rick (Wagoner) to take another look at the Cadillac truck question," Jack said, as we moved into one of the small press briefing rooms on the Opel stand. "The rest is up to you."

I'm sure I fumbled through some sort of thank you and said I'd take it from there, but the whole idea of a Cadillac truck had been a non-starter in GM North America since the day I had arrived. Super-grateful, lost in thought, but incredibly pumped, I walked on air back to the Cadillac stand.

Still, getting a Cadillac SUV past the BrandScape palace guards would no doubt be a battle royale.

The Scape of Things to Come!

The BrandScape vehicle market and brand positioning

assessment was approved by the GM North American Strategy Board in 1996. This work was certainly needed to resolve overlap between the marketing divisions, make better use of GM resources, and hopefully, produce more distinctive and profitable products. However, BrandScape was all about better separating GM from their sixty-plus models, and *not at all* about reducing the number of divisions to some lower number where meaningful product differentiation and impactful marketing could be achieved.

Truly, an opportunity missed.

More disconcerting to me was BrandScape's conclusion that Cadillac would sell only luxury *cars*—period. With GMC in the portfolio and already selling more premium versions of comparable Chevrolet products, any luxury trucks GM might develop in the future would be sold under the GMC brand.

Wait! What?

It really wasn't very likely that high-end customers would drive to Mercedes, BMW, *and* Pontiac/GMC stores to comparison shop for a luxury SUV. Luxury is image, and GMC, albeit perceived as being above Chevrolet, didn't have that kind of cache at the time. Limiting Cadillac to luxury cars had to be especially disappointing to my predecessor, John Grettenberger, who first proposed a Cadillac SUV in 1995 and was denied.

In early 1997, when meeting with the Cadillac team and key dealers across the country, it was clear that Cadillac was already losing loyal customers to luxury brands with trucks and might soon fall behind Lincoln as well, which would launch its Navigator in a few months. Once lost, luxury vehicle owners are hard to get back since many enjoy great service from the other brands. Most of Cadillac's customer base was in the hands of its single-point dealers, not so much in showrooms shared with GMC where a Yukon Denali *might* keep a Cadillac customer in the GM fold.

While there were many reasons to believe GM would be leaving money on the table by limiting Cadillac to just passenger cars, BrandScape concluded otherwise—a decision that had less to do with luxury customers' sense of self and more to do with attempting to optimize a failing go-to-market strategy featuring too many divisional brands.

Meanwhile, Back in Detroit....

Back in Detroit, at the conclusion of the first Cadillac staff meeting following the Frankfurt Motor Show, I asked Pete Gerosa and Martin Walsh to remain in the room and shut the door. They looked at one another as if they were in trouble.

"We have a shot at a truck," I said, and went on to share what Jack Smith had told me. Getting approval for such a vehicle would be a challenge—we would certainly have limited funds to work with, and we could count on a mother lode of internal resistance to the idea. We needed a knowledgeable, resourceful, and scrappy Cadillac brand manager who could work with the full-size truck team in putting together a proposal. We agreed it should be Steve Hill, who joined us a few minutes later.

As we began to discuss vehicle size (whether it should be similar to the Tahoe or Suburban), and how to differentiate it from Chevrolet and GMC versions, it occurred to me that various internal interests would work overtime to undermine the business case, which would kill the program. That said, we might have an ace up our sleeve—the financial staff would likely assume the same dealer discount as used by Chevy and GMC full-size trucks, which was around 18 percent at the time. Cadillac's more expensive vehicles carried a lower dealer discount of 11 percent. I instructed Steve to let the 18 percent assumption ride until just before senior management reviewed the program, then sign up for the usual Cadillac discount level, adding considerable profit to the business case and confining the final debate to the strategic merits of a Cadillac truck.

Michael Grimaldi

That night, Michael Grimaldi called. He was GM's full-size truck vehicle line executive and would be responsible for developing the Cadillac SUV proposal. Over the years, we had worked together several times. We knew one another well and he was reaching out for my thoughts, but he was also in a bind.

"I'm not supposed to talk to you," Michael said. He had been instructed to work on this project without involving the Cadillac team. This was disappointing news, and also unrealistic. We were relatively old hands in product development and valued each other's thoughts. More importantly, how could the "voice of the customer," Cadillac, *not* have a seat at the table? Cadillac marketing had plowed this ground before, and we had plenty of insight into the nascent luxury truck market.

I told Michael about the conversation with Jack Smith and that Cadillac had already developed some initial thoughts. Steve Hill would be ready to work with Michael's team first thing the next morning. We also discussed the limited resources available—about $10 million for engineering and capital combined, a tiny amount in auto-land—and the need to decide pretty quickly on the short (Tahoe) or long (Suburban) wheelbase to use.

We also discussed what might be unique to a Cadillac truck, since money and time did not permit much in the way of visual specifics. OnStar offered one such possibility; they had second-generation hardware in development that eliminated the klutzy and freestanding handset (which customers didn't want and dealers had difficulty installing), using a tidy, three-button-equipped rearview mirror with microphones built into the vehicle's headliner—all factory installed for a high-quality result. With Chet Huber's help at OnStar, the launch of the Escalade—pretty much last to market in its segment—had a neat, much-discussed, first-to-market infotainment feature! OnStar uses this same basic user interface to this day… more than twenty years later!

After the call with Michael, I thought about him being instructed not to engage Cadillac. It was silly, petty even, but perhaps indicative of the lengths the system was willing to go to put the kibosh on the idea of a Cadillac truck. I resolved to talk with Ron Zarrella the next day at the quarterly GM North America leadership meeting.

At that meeting, during the mid-morning break, I saw Ron was alone for a moment. I walked up to him, told him how excited the Cadillac team was about the possibility of an SUV, and handed him a note I had typed the night before that summarized the points I had shared with Michael. As I quickly highlighted the main points, Ron didn't say much, although his flushed skin suggested he wasn't a happy camper.

Crunch Time

For the next few weeks, work on a Cadillac SUV progressed on several fronts. Designer Terry Henline was developing the exterior and interior specifics, using the GMC Yukon as a starting point, but with precious few degrees of freedom. In fact, Wayne Cherry to this day describes the first Escalade's uniqueness as, "Just a grille and small badging." Still, Terry's exterior proposal *was* distinctive: spare but tasteful. The front end was a simple, large chrome oval, with the Cadillac wreath and crest set against a matte black grille insert. Unique chrome wheels were found, and the brand name *Cadillac* was applied in large block letters to the front doors on both sides (at about eye level for those in passenger cars!). Interior differences were limited to Cadillac-specific leather seating materials, Cadillac ornamentation, and the new three-button On-Star application. Despite this limited Cadillac uniqueness, Terry had developed an attractive SUV and one Bob Lutz would often say was his favorite among all generations of 'Slade. (Figure 1)

Michael's team was closely following Terry's work, interpreting the design into engineering requirements, supplier development, assembly plant capacity, tooling, and developing the all-important business case with finance. Lots of internal arguments took place and the GM market analysis crew, which was fiercely independent, was lobbied hard by both Cadillac and opposing forces inside of GM North America. Remarkably, there was radio silence from the Chevrolet and GMC divisions' management, whose brands exclusively represented GM in the SUV business at the time.

As the proposal came together, the business case was positive, but conservative sales volume assumptions made it only marginally so—at which point, we laid Cadillac's lower dealer discount on the table, and the program's return on investment became *really* attractive.

Now that we had an economic no-brainer, the gloves came off!

Showdown

Following a Strategy Board meeting in late October, Rick Wagoner called another meeting to review the Cadillac

SUV proposal. Ron Zarrella was there, along with the heads of planning, manufacturing, engineering, design, and purchasing. I was also there with Michael Grimaldi and Mike DiGiovanni (aka MickeyD) who led GM's Market Analysis team. I had collected my thoughts about the merits of a decision to move forward and my assistant, Diane Rowader, had typed them up that morning. Michael presented the program scope, investment, timing, and attractive business case. MickeyD discussed the segment sales volume opportunity and what we were beginning to understand about luxury vehicle owners' interest in SUVs and their related brand rankings. It was all good news for Cadillac.

But we had to deal with BrandScape, for whom a Cadillac truck was decidedly off strategy.

On this point, Wagoner solicited input from those around the table. Rick was two seats to my left, and Ron was between us. Rick started with the person to my right and went around the room. By the time Rick got to himself, the input was largely no go, with Michael Grimaldi and Mike DiGiovanni favoring the project but the functional leaders opposing, ostensibly based on BrandScape.

Wagoner passed, wanting to hear everyone else's views, at which point Zarrella argued against the proposal. This was no surprise since BrandScape was his baby.

Talking last, I went through my points—the positive business case, the rapid growth in the segment, the loss of loyal Cadillac owners to other luxury makes offering SUVs, and a Cadillac SUV as a meaningful first opportunity to show consumers something really different was happening at a brand otherwise seen as increasingly irrelevant and in decline.

After a brief pause, Wagoner thanked everyone for the quick work done by the various teams over the preceding six weeks. Rick thought the next thing to do was share the status with Jack Smith later that afternoon. Rick would do so and asked Ron Zarrella to come along. When I left the conference room, I called Diane and asked her to fax a copy of my arguments to Jack's office. I wanted him to have the benefit of thoughts, complete and unfiltered.

"For" It Is!

That evening, I got a call from Ron at home. It was among the shortest conversations we would ever have, something along the lines of "You got your truck." That was truly great news, and I told him how excited the Cadillac dealers would be. I told him we would organize a satellite broadcast to inform the dealers, and I invited him to join. This was "hope" on steroids, and I wanted him to hear their enthusiasm and gratitude firsthand. Ron declined, and with the passage of time, it seemed to have been an opportunity missed for him to accumulate some goodwill with some of GM's best and most influential dealers.

Over the years, I have imagined the meeting in Jack's office—him listening to Wagoner's summary, shaded neither for nor against. Zarrella no doubt reminding Smith of the prior year's BrandScape decisions. Smith nodding, but probably noting Lincoln's early success with the Navigator, feedback he was getting directly from Cadillac dealers, etc. Jack Smith was happiest when folks made the right decision on their own, but he had zero problem leading a horse to water.

Say What?

The next day, I got the assignment to tell Roy Roberts, then general manager of Pontiac and GMC, that Cadillac was approved for a full-size SUV based on the GMC Yukon. He was not happy. The approval of this first Escalade guaranteed that Cadillac would be part of the all-new full-size SUV program that would launch in a little more than two years. Any second-generation vehicle would also have more visual and technical features unique to Cadillac. Roy no doubt believed a Cadillac SUV could limit the GMC Yukon's sales volume and market share, and possibly also his division's profits.

Roy was resolved to reverse the decision, but his arguments fell on deaf ears. That ship had sailed.

Hope 1.0

In early November, we arranged a satellite broadcast to inform Cadillac dealers of the news. Nothing was disclosed in the invitation. Pete Gerosa opened the broadcast, totally in character as the gruff, no-nonsense, sometimes profane sales leader he truly was. (Nobody, but nobody, picked his pocket. And no one enjoyed more respect or success among their peers for developing people than Pete.) I told the dealers we had an SUV program and shared some but not all of the details. We would launch in ten months but, as a consequence, uniqueness would be limited. Still, they could use that information to their advantage, persuading customers who wanted a truck to hold on. And, once in the full-size SUV program, subsequent generations would have more "Cadillac" content.

There was a tsunami of positive energy during the call, for this first tangible down payment on hope!

My Name Is 'Slade

Vehicle naming is usually the province of the brand, and we often consult history to see if we own names we can consider. In this case, there weren't any. Working with the usual suspects (i.e., ad agencies, legal, etc.), several names were developed, including Escalade. On the surface, the name seemed to convey something rising, which would certainly be true since Cadillac would be coming from nowhere in entering the growing luxury SUV market. The word is actually French, meaning the scaling of fortified ramparts, itself a nice, competitive allegory. And it was a tip of the cap to Antoine de la Mothe Cadillac, the French explorer who founded Detroit in 1701.

At times, it can seem like GM has a lot of naming experts. While the Cadillac team liked the name a lot, and Terry Henline literally turned the name into a larger-than-life billboard on the vehicle's front doors, other parties in GM thought the name either garish or too difficult to pronounce. Sticking to our guns, Escalade was chosen—at least until many of its owners shortened it to just plain 'Slade!

The Rest of the Story

For the $10 million invested in the original Escalade, GM salted away approximately $200 million in pre-tax profit during the first-generation Escalade's brief, two-year life. The second generation was more substantial in engineering and capital expenditures, but so was the level of specificity. We wanted/needed more horsepower, a better driveline, bigger wheels and tires, unique body and interior styling, and other chassis technology improvements. Everything was either better or bigger or bolder, including the wreath and crest!

One afternoon, Wayne Cherry invited me to the Cadillac design studio to look at the full-size clay model of the second-generation Escalade. Carl Sewell was visiting Detroit at the time and came along. As we walked around to the rear of the vehicle, we saw a designer experimenting with different size wreath and crest badges for the tailgate.

Standing back about thirty feet, the first design applied seemed too small, if not lost in the big canvas that was 'Slade's backside.

We went a little bigger, then bigger again. It seemed we were nearing the size of a Frisbee! And while the larger scale certainly worked better in relation to the rear hatch proportions, it was also clear the size of the wreath and crest *itself* was a kind of message—and totally consistent with the confidence, the attitude we wanted to bring back that had once separated Cadillac from other luxury marques. It was an all-American, larger-than-life expression, unafraid to be seen and not cloaked in the kind of cultural understatement and/or conformity offered at the time by German and Japanese imports.

And so the second generation 'Slade launched with a *very* prominent wreath and crest fore and aft, stirring the pot once more both outside and inside the company. A senior

executive confided that he was distressed with the garish-
ness of the jewelry on the vehicle. I couldn't agree but, to
be fair, he wasn't especially close to customers in his work,
certainly not as close as one of Cadillac's biggest dealers,
John Lund. In his Phoenix dealership, Lund was ordering
the outsized wreath and crest from GM's service parts organization and using it to customize other Cadillac vehicles in his inventory!

Jukebox

Serendipity sometimes plays a role in success, and it did
with 'Slade. We certainly didn't foresee its rapid accent
to cult classic in our early projections. True, Cadillac was
deeply embedded in the American psyche, with well over
200 songs featuring Cadillac, including by artists like Are-
tha Franklin, The Stray Cats, Bruce Springsteen, and Don
Henley.

When Escalade was launched, we played to its unapolo-
getic boldness by using George Thorogood's "Bad to the
Bone" anthem. America embraced 'Slade's attitude as it
took over as the preferred canvas for the vast customizing automotive sub-culture in the United States. No better
place to witness the customizing craze 'Slade tapped into
than the annual automotive orgy that is SEMA (Specialty
Equipment Market Association) in Las Vegas. A new wave
of Cadillac-flavored tunes began hitting the airwaves, with
athletes, artists, black car (limousine) operations, and the
generally wealthy gravitating to the substance and image
that the Escalade possessed.

Earle Eldridge wrote an article for *USA Today* entitled,
"Escalade Scores with Athletes, Rappers," in October 2001,
following the launch of the second-generation Escalade.
He noted the Escalade was attracting owners twelve years
younger with 25 percent bigger incomes than the typical
Cadillac owner. Top draft picks were buying 'Slades with

their signing bonuses, and musicians were featuring the vehicle in their lyrics and stagecraft. Some music videos looked like Escalade commercials, with Ludacris' "Southern Hospitality" featuring slow, lingering camera shots along the side, ending up focusing on the rear emblem— the same one we couldn't make big enough in the design studio!

Cash Machine

With the Escalade, Cadillac began to enjoy some serious improvements in profitability, which made other pending investments in the brand (like the all-new rear-wheel drive architecture for CTS and STS) risks worth taking. At some point in the second generation's lifecycle, the Escalade became the second most profitable GM model (behind Corvette), produced the majority of Cadillac's profits, and consistently attracted a new, wealthier, and more youthful audience to the brand.

The third generation Escalade, with even more distinctive styling and features than before, further broadened Cadillac's reach and became the "killer app" in the segment. Powerful, quiet, and composed, the third generation Escalade was a technological tour de force—and was priced accordingly. More profits followed. (Figure 2)

I recall Rick Wagoner once observing that it was better to have a good product in a great segment than a great product in a good segment. Escalade is certainly proof of that as the first generation 'Slade gave Cadillac (and GM) a toehold into a market that, over time, has generated huge profits.

Another moral to the Escalade story is: Best to market *can* trump first to market! Hats off to GM's truck engineering crew for this result and for seizing on Escalade as the canvas for some of their best work ever.

CHAPTER 3

ART & SCIENCE

E scalade plugged a rapidly growing hole in Cadillac's portfolio and was a huge profit and morale booster for its dealers and for GM. But it was but a bridge to something more encompassing, durable, and compelling—a reimagining of Cadillac that traded on its rich history but built for tomorrow.

The Cadillac team devoted nearly all of 1997 to reimagining Cadillac, managed by the diminutive but passionate Peter Levin. We had various internal partners in this effort, including trench-level folks from engineering (GM still had a small cadre of development engineers working exclusively on Cadillac products), and Mike DiGiovanni's team in market analysis. None, however, were more essential or more valuable than Wayne Cherry and his design staff team.

As noted earlier, Cherry had spent twenty-six years living and working for GM in Europe, pretty much the center of the world when it comes to all things luxury, and not just automobiles. His time in Europe, first at Vauxhall and later at Opel, made him a proponent of dedicated brand character studios, which he installed for GM's US brands once he returned to Detroit and became vice president of design. He was used to working in places where design and marketing personnel could collaborate on vehicle design—nay, perhaps even a brand's overall positioning in the market.

Until I arrived on the scene, with Cadillac badly in need of a major tune-up, too few of the other marketing division leaders, including my predecessor at times, took Cherry up on his offer to work together. Brand management further complicated the potential for collaboration since "brand" meant any one of the sixty-plus models GM had on the market at the time. Sadly, many brand managers wanted little or nothing to do with their divisional motherships, making design staff's outreach more difficult.

To sort through what would become Cadillac's Art & Science brand positioning strategy, we needed Cherry and his design team's talent, insight, and creativity. Our collective "push" for dramatic change probably came at a time when there was considerable "pull" for something new and different from GM's leadership. Suffice it to say that having both made it easier to make a big change but, as will be noted later, the "pull" was sometimes halting, as if beset with doubts that any amount of investment in Cadillac would make a difference.

Wayne and I, and our teams, had our work cut out for us.

Trends

We started our reimagining work by looking inward at the brand's history and what had made it unique and successful for most of Cadillac's first century. Styling was a big part of this, but the brand also boasted a long and well-documented list of technological firsts, with some relatively recent new installments in the form of electronic fuel injection, electronic traction control, and StabiliTrak stability control.

Setting Cadillac's history aside, we made a concerted effort to look at how the luxury vehicle market had evolved. It was clear Europe's command of all things luxury (watches, apparel, etc.) was influencing the rising sales of Mercedes and BMW vehicles in the US, to Cadillac's detriment. Performance and quality had always been relative advantages of European luxury imports. Like other goods categories, the noble marques seemed to have mastered the details in their vehicles, reinforcing perceptions of quality and crafts-manship. Increasingly, their vehicles were also beginning to feature leading-edge technologies.

Ironically, technology was an area where *America* excelled, especially in computers, space, and military applications—areas of growing interest to many luxury vehicle consumers. Cadillac was once among the innovators in the vehicle business, and it certainly needed to revive that image in ways meaningful to consumers. Perhaps we could do so by leveraging *both* Cadillac and America's technological reputations. Perhaps Cadillac's new styling, hopefully bold and uniquely American in expressiveness, could visually *communicate* such technological values.

Importantly, we also looked outward at the likely trajectory of industry growth, at changing segmentation in the luxury vehicle market, and the mix of different body styles within those segments. We also considered the megatrends expected to affect everyone and everything, with a focus on those trends most expected to define future luxury vehicle consumers. Personal safety, being entertained and/or staying connected, concern for the environment, an appreciation for details, and the appearance of craftsmanship were all standout areas of interest and concern.

Zarrella, Cherry, and I also visited Harley Davidson and discussed the whys and wherefores of their very successful brand repositioning. They, too, took time to understand and leverage their rich history in reimagining their brand, but in a way that was respectful of modern-day sensibilities. The 1960s (think *Easy Rider*) were of great historical significance for Harley Davidson, and their revival in the 1990s unashamedly celebrated this bit of their past to great effect. In contrast, the best decade for Cadillac was the 1950s. All things considered, in this decade, Cadillac was hitting on all cylinders when it came to packing styling and technology into "gotta have" vehicles, one after another!

Journalistas 1.0

We also spent time with select automotive media getting their unique point of view as they drove, evaluated, and critiqued a never-ending stream of new models. "Buff books" (as in "car buffs") are especially influential to luxury vehicle consumers and what they buy, and we wanted journalists to feel they were an integral part of our inquiry and journey. If they somehow felt included in this work, perhaps they might round up in their reviews of future Cadillac models.

The first media outreach took place in the *Cadillac Collection* in mid-1997—the brand's museum and archives located in Warren, Michigan. Beautiful historic vehicles, technology and engine displays, signage, catalogues, owner records, etc. were all there, carefully managed by Greg Wallace, the collection's curator (and a noted go-to fellow among the world's vehicle restoration community). The

Collection was a deep soak in Cadillac's accomplishments over 100 years and my predecessor, John Grettenberger, gave me his key to the collection, noting he would sometimes visit after hours to reflect on what once was…and what again might be.

We had invited fifteen to twenty journalists for pizza and beer, whom we encouraged to write notes and/or questions on the paper tablecloths as we talked them through our work-in-progress repositioning thoughts. While we had not decided to go with Art & Science *per se*, and didn't have any future product visuals to share, the rough outlines of change were on the table—a return to dramatic styling, a return to best-possible driving dynamics through rear-wheel drive architectures, and a focus on select technologies and the emerging, post-Boomer luxury consumer.

This was an off-the-record event, which overcame some

of the inherent reluctance of journalists sitting together in on-the-record events from making comments or asking questions that might disclose their working storylines. The beer might have helped overcome those inhibitions and aided in an energetic give-and-take that evening. By night's end, we felt we had tested the basic premise of a new Cadillac for the first time with an especially learned and discriminating external audience—and we came away with support for our ambitions and respect for our candor.

Robbing the Cradle

As we sifted through all this information, and before deciding on too many specifics of a reimagined Cadillac, it was important to honestly consider with whom our more promising opportunities lay. On this point, it seemed unlikely that anything Cadillac might do would bring so many Boomers already driving other luxury marques (Benz, BMW, Lexus) back to Cadillac. They were excellent cars, sold and serviced by excellent dealers, and totally reinforced most luxury consumers' self-images. They were fun to drive and fun to be seen in!

The next generation of luxury vehicle buyers, however, were another matter. Gen Xers weren't yet as established in the luxury market and didn't have so many preconceived notions about luxury brands—and in the world of cars, kids don't typically drive what their parents drove!

We weren't going to give up on anyone, of course, but we decided our principal audience, the one that would inform our choices, was the post-Boomer crowd.

The "Science" Part

With the post-Boomer target audience in mind, and having fished the megatrend ocean, five attributes stood out as core elements of Art & Science, more specifically the "Science" part. First and foremost, Cadillac needed to return to rear-wheel-drive (RWD) architecture for its passenger cars. While Cadillac's engineering crew had done an admirable job over the years wringing better and better performance from the brand's front-wheel-drive (FWD) models, they fell short of the ride and handling that Mercedes and BMW had obtained with their RWD offerings. Front-to-back weight distribution was better, and there was no torque steer when accelerating, i.e., the annoying bit of lurch, usually to the right of center, typical of FWD vehicles. RWD is also the preferred configuration for any performance variants, like AMG at Mercedes or BMW's M-series—something our team aspired to do as well.

Importantly, RWD gives designers better proportions to work with when styling a vehicle, most significantly eliminating the longer front-bumper overhangs of FWD (think Platypus), and enabling the vehicle's four wheels to be pulled to the corners. Moving to RWD offered an additional benefit, allowing Cadillac once again to have a vehicle architecture it did not share with other GM models and, hence, engineered exclusively for the luxury market.

The second, third, and fourth desired vehicle attributes were about all-weather control, active safety, and infotainment. It was clear to us that luxury consumers were showing interest in all-wheel drive passenger cars, not just in trucks and SUVs. It was also clear that *active* safety technologies were gaining traction. Features that help avoid accidents, like StabiliTrak, lane departure warnings, etc. were of increasing interest in addition to the usual *passive* safety features, like seat belts, air bags, and seat belt tensioners, which are all about surviving an accident.

As for in-vehicle infotainment, it was in its early days in 1997, but Bose was a long-time Cadillac partner and be-

We needed to think in terms of *attitude* again, thought-fully calibrated for the tastes of our target audience (and the forty years of ever-more specific occupant safety and emissions regulations enacted since 1959!).

The "Art" Part

Design saw it the same way, especially the notion of Cadillac celebrating America's culture and technological prowess. Millennials and Gen Xers were growing up with many areas of American accomplishment and excellence, like computers and space exploration. It was their world. The look and feel of their daily lives and their surroundings were different from those of their Boomer parents, and they were quite comfortable with it all.

Cherry's team believed a new Cadillac design language or form vocabulary could be hewn from these exposures and preferences, offering our target audience styling they might call their own—styling as if designed by a computer, edgy, sheer, angular like a Stealth Fighter jet.

Now that would be daring, celebrating both America's modern-day technological prowess and its underlying spirit of innovation—a design language visually *communicating* Cadillac's technological values, but one also filled with *attitude*.

Cherry worked with his team to put together a representative form vocabulary for future Cadillac models. It would be the brand's visual signature, showing how elements like front and rear lighting, grilles, feature lines on exterior panels, interior details like seat sew patterns, placement of wood appointments (with focus on areas the passengers touch), badging, etc., would be executed. (Figure 4 and 5)

This form vocabulary would be used in some way across all models in the product portfolio. Early on, no particular vehicle existed to apply these elements on since it would be a few months before taking the complete Art & Science strategy to the North American Strategy Board, the decision-making body for GM's North American business and product portfolio, including Cadillac. Still, it was very clear that this new form vocabulary was modern, taut and athletic, while also being unique and bold!

Along the way to Cadillac's new design language, and to dispel concerns that such edgy designs might be inherently off-putting, Cherry's team did their own homework on the notion of beauty because, usually, ugly cars don't enjoy much or lasting success. A range of design executions across various luxury product categories—watches, jets, and apparel—were compared. (Figure 6)

It was easy to see that *beauty* covered a lot of ground and that two very different looking jets, the handsome Gulfstream and the angular Stealth Fighter, were both attractive. The luxury world already appreciated and embraced a wide range of designs, and it gave the Cadillac team confidence that we could *and would* be successful with the new Art & Science design language.

Showtime!

By February 1998, the Cadillac/design staff team had completed its year-long brand repositioning work and was ready to present it for approval at the monthly North American Strategy Board meeting. We would do so at GM's historic Design Dome, the centerpiece of Saarinen's GM Technical Center architectural tour de force in Warren, Michigan, where there was plenty of room to spread out. Cherry remembers the occasion as the biggest Dome show he was ever a part of. We would use a couple of handfuls of twenty-foot-long display boards to present the analysis and conclusions underpinning Art & Science. Around the interior perimeter of the circular dome, Cherry positioned the oversized boards, collectively displaying a future product portfolio sporting the new design language, including full-size side views for all models along with some front and rear images. The most important future model illustrated in this fashion was a next-generation Catera, or what would become the CTS.

There were some instrument panel and other interior illustrations as well to give the Strategy Board a complete look at what it would mean to the customer, at least visually. Notably, the center part of future Cadillac instrument panels looked like a high-end computer tower, topped with an LCD screen. In keeping with the importance of craftsmanship to luxury vehicle owners, a lovely analog timepiece was also featured in the center stack. Ultimately, Cadillac fashioned a partnership with BVLGARI for this important detail.

We had the full attention of the Strategy Board that morn-

ing, and they had many questions, comments, and opinions. Without question, the new styling direction got very
close inspection since it was quite a departure from current Cadillacs. One-level-down product attributes like
all-weather control and active safety were understood and
agreed to, although the alternate propulsion discussion
was considered wine-before-its-time and tabled. While
the Cadillac design crew had lived with Art & Science
for the better part of a year, this was a *lot* for the Strategy
Board to consider.

And Art & Science was an all-or-nothing proposition.
It was not only a wholesale change in the look and feel
of Cadillac, but a significant investment in a new rear-
wheel-drive architecture that would underpin more than
half of the brand's product portfolio and require a new
US assembly plant.

As the morning session concluded, the Strategy Board

seemed persuaded by what they saw, but they had a full afternoon ahead of them, including a review of a Catera replacement program. Like the in-market Catera, the replacement would be based on the Opel Omega which, while appropriate for its position in the European market, wasn't anywhere close in refinement and performance to Mercedes or BMW and a mile away from the Art & Science design language.

To its credit, that afternoon the Strategy Board rejected the Catera replacement program and formally endorsed the Art & Science strategy. Some found it compelling, while others may have simply concluded that doing something different was better than staying the course. Rick Wagoner seemed to cover both views in an *Automotive News* interview in September 2003:

> *It (Art & Science) was clearly one that challenged people. While it was sort of shocking in its boldness, it was*

upon reflection something that fit. It felt right.

A few months later, in June 1998, at one of its regular meetings, GM's Board of Directors received a detailed marketing update, including a status report on the positioning of each of the divisional brands. John Smale, GM's lead director, said after the session:

> *It provides clear evidence that everyone is thinking the right way about product positioning. Cadillac was the clearest example of that.*

Having abandoned the Opel-based Catera replacement, the Strategy Board requested the urgent development of a new vehicle design based on the Art & Science illustrations they had seen during the morning review...and by urgent, they meant in no more than *ninety days*—light speed by GM standards!

It took four years before this vehicle, based as it was on a new rear-wheel-drive architecture and built in a new assembly plant, would be introduced, such being the lead times typical in the auto industry.

But there would be much to do in the meantime—selling current products to be sure, getting ready for the Escalade launch, integrating Art & Science into every other aspect of Cadillac's go-to-market activities, and engaging the media about the big changes to come.

On this last point, next to Escalade, Evoq (pronounced evoke) would turn out to be the biggest lever we could pull in capturing the public's attention.

Chapter 4

Evoq...Cadillac's Coming—Out Party!

hile Wayne Cherry organized his troops to deal with the Strategy Board's ninety-day challenge on a Catera replacement, we began to discuss how and when to communicate Cadillac's new direction to dealers, media, and the public. All of these audiences needed hope of one kind or another, and it was clearly in our interest to construct and deliver the messages rather than have the media fill into the vacuum. We had current products to sell, and we needed the dealers' best efforts on this, on improving their facilities and personnel, and on keeping Cadillac's loyal owners in tow for as long as possible.

Concept cars are a tried-and-true means in the auto industry for gaining attention. Some do it when there are no
new models to introduce, but many do it to signal a new
addition to their portfolio or that a current model—perhaps the brand itself—will undergo significant change.

Art & Science would certainly be a big change at Cadillac,
a tailor-made assignment for a concept car. Of course, in
the ever-centralizing GM environment, such efforts sometimes attracted undue internal interest, so we resolved to
plan and execute our concept car with some care. Asking
for forgiveness seemed more prudent than asking for per-
mission.

The important call to make was the type of concept car
we should develop. We certainly discussed a CTS concept, one that would be somewhat different from its final
production shape. The industry sometimes describes this
as "cheating," meaning the concept car might sit lower,
maybe featuring a wider track, a different side profile, a

bit of a slammed roof, etc. Such behavior was common in concept-car land, especially if the concept related to an in-market vehicle.

Wayne was very much in favor of a two-seat convertible. In the luxury market, such products, like the Mercedes SL, are among a given brand's most exclusive, most personal, most highly styled, and highest price offerings. While unit sales are among the lowest, such vehicles are coveted by consumers and media alike.

Since Art & Science was *all* about style, check that box— the Cadillac Evoq concept car was born! If Escalade was about stemming Cadillac's decline, Evoq would signal the return of America's most storied luxury automotive brand.

Who Pays?

The next issue was money. Concept cars aren't cheap, especially those that can actually be driven—think in terms of at least $1 million for a running concept car, and certainly more now. Design had no budget for concept cars, per se, and no slush funds large enough to absorb one. Evoq would necessarily fall to Cadillac to fund, which seemed entirely reasonable since it was part-in-parcel brand messaging.

Finding $1 million for a concept car in an $8 billion car company should have been relatively easy to do, but it wasn't. A study had just been launched on consolidating various back-office sales and marketing activities of the divisional brands—things like media buying, racing programs, promotions, dealer development, etc. This study went by the acronym FMIT (Field and Marketing Integration Team), and it would run its course over most of 1998 and be implemented on January 1, 1999. More on that later.

The practical effect of FMIT was that, early on in the study, some folks were already rooting around to understand the kinds of divisional spendings that might fall into centralized hands…and beginning to assemble the grist for a business case for the proposed consolidations. Evoq survived such inquiries through some thoughtful and creative work by the not-yet-consolidated Cadillac finance team, with the total expenditure ultimately spread over a number of different line items.

When and Where?

While some car companies do concept cars in house, a cottage industry of sorts specializes in building such vehicles. Wayne suggested we use Metalcrafters based in California. It was close to a small, advanced Design Staff outpost that Wayne used for special projects. Wayne selected Kip Wasenko to lead the work from Detroit, but he used the California team to engage daily on the details with Metalcrafters. Proceeding in this manner allowed us to cloak the Evoq project for several months.

We targeted the North American International Auto Show (NAIAS) in Detroit in January 1999 as the time and place of Evoq's public debut. It was Cadillac's hometown and, despite every expectation of lousy weather in Detroit that time of year, it was nonetheless a well-attended venue by global car companies and international media alike.

We also held open the possibility of teasing out Evoq's forthcoming NAIAS debut to our select journalist group at the Pebble Beach Concours in August 1998. Wayne and I had visited the Concours the prior year, and we felt this annual celebration of the world's best historic vehicles would be a great platform for Cadillac events. Wayne was well known to the Concours organization, having served as a judge there since 1995. (Cherry would remain a judge through 2019!) After the Strategy Board's approval of Art & Science, it seemed to be an especially attractive venue—and point in time—to discuss Art & Science with our journalist friends. If we did so in August, we could show a little leg as to what it all meant for future Cadillac styling with some kind of limited Evoq reveal.

This was all food for thought since it was early March, and Evoq's development had miles to go!

More Importantly, What?

For sure, Evoq would be a bold and distinctive design, taking the new Art & Science form vocabulary to the limit. Front and rear overhangs were quite short, and the car featured a long dash-to-axle profile typical of classic sports cars. Neon lighting elements were employed in Evoq's rear end, not only for a more striking and uniform appearance when on, but also for its faster "on" characteristic viz incandescent lighting elements...certainly better for anyone trying to follow an Evoq too closely!

As a two-passenger coupe, it would be powerful, fitted with a supercharged Northstar V-8 with continuously-variable valve timing. And it would showcase a host of advanced technologies—Night Vision, updated StabiliTrak, run-flat tires, rear obstacle detection, rear vision cameras replacing outside mirrors, and Communiport (a mobile multimedia information system with voice-activated navigation, electronic mail, and entertainment features). It would have a one-button retractable hardtop, bronzed glass, and no exterior door handles. (A key fob would both unlock and slightly open the doors.) To provide reassuring structure while driving top up or top down, the drivable Evoq would use hydroformed rails running front to back on both sides of the vehicle's chassis.

Inside and out, Evoq would communicate everything Cadillac had in mind with Art & Science.

Internal Scrum

By early summer, Wayne Cherry and I felt the car was coming along nicely. It would certainly be ready for the North American International Auto Show (NAIAS) in Detroit in January, and we got comfortable with the idea of including *some* representation of Evoq in the Art & Science briefing that had been organized for select media at Pebble Beach, California, in August. Evoq would be about deeds, not words, and sharing the concept car with the journalists in some way would no doubt help build awareness for and excitement about Evoq's public debut five months later.

News of Cadillac's planned media event at Pebble Beach got the attention of various GM executives, and not just corporate public relations. Not surprisingly, Chevrolet feared Evoq would encroach on its uber-profitable Corvette. The Corvette vehicle line executive responsible for all Bowling Green assembly plant products demanded a number of changes to the concept car as if it were destined to become a production program.

Uh…no.

Evoq was a *concept* car, its sole purpose being to communicate Art & Science to the public for the first time. It needed to be pure and without compromise. Cadillac was paying the bill, having shorted other budgeted areas in order to build it. With Wayne Cherry and Kip Wasenko, Cadillac would make any and all calls about Evoq's design and content—for the last time, it turns out, as the FMIT consolidation took concept car decisions away from the marketing divisions for good beginning in 1999.

Journalistas 2.0

The August 1998 media gathering at Pebble Beach included many of the same people who first participated in the session at the Cadillac Collection the prior year. This time, we would share the details of Art & Science, our target audience, the influences in their lives, the technology we believed most interested them, and the new Cadillac design language. We touched broadly on other related changes to come, like the logo and naming conventions. While we couldn't get specific on the product portfolio, we could confirm a new entry-luxury segment entry that would replace Catera in "a few years."

And we shared our plan to encapsulate the meaning of Art & Science for the public with a concept car to debut at NAIAS the following January. We described the vehicle simply as a two-passenger roadster and offered but a glimpse—a front three-quarter view of a mostly draped Evoq showing only the new-design-language headlamp. This photo had the added virtue of being a touch grainy, as if taken using a Brownie camera in a dim garage!

It was most unsatisfying, and groans ensued, but it would have to do until January. As it turned out, this bit of tease became a great shared memory for many of the journalists.

January 1999 NAIAS

Most big motor shows reserve a few days for the media and suppliers before opening to the public. During these days, most auto companies schedule press conferences to introduce new models or concept cars. Cadillac would do the same at the January 1999 NAIAS. For the press event, the usual display of multiple production models was removed and replaced by a purpose-built, hub-and-spoke, raised stand. The hub was at the back of the display space, and just two spokes radiated at slight angles to the front right and front left of the display. Seating for the journalists and other attendees (Cadillac, Design, GM corporate, competitors) was between the two spokes.

A turntable was in the center of the front hub and turntables at the ends of the two spokes. Art & Science was intentional about leveraging Cadillac's rich history, and we put two great two-seaters from the brand's past on those turntables, building a kind of bridge between the old and the new.

On one spoke was the 1953 Le Mans (introduced at a GM Motorama event) and on the other was the 1959 Cyclone (itself a show car). Both vehicles received a lot of TLC ahead of NAIAS from Cadillac Collection's Director, Greg Wallace, and repainted using the same Argentanium pewter finish featured on Evoq. It was going to be a great family reunion with all participants wearing the same T-shirt!

Before the reveal, Evoq was backstage, as were Jack Smith and Rick Wagoner. They were thrilled with the car, seeing it in the flesh for the first time, and probably with the progress being made at Cadillac as well. If they had heard any internal grousing about Evoq along the way, it wasn't showing.

After some introductory remarks about a changing Cadillac and Art & Science, Wayne Cherry presided over the reveal—and Evoq rolled into view and onto the turntable. (Figure 7)

It was truly an electric moment—the car was radiant in the show lighting, rakish and aggressive, *very* new, and *very* different. Cadillac was doing something unexpected—but also something totally consistent with its history. As Cherry noted, "Evoq is a bold statement. It is immediately identifiable as a Cadillac."

The Evoq was greeted with a lot of applause, hoots, and hollers, which lasted for a good while. It felt like one giant, "It's about time, Cadillac; we've missed you!"

Mission Accomplished

Some people wondered if we could possibly be serious about the Evoq's chiseled looks, including skeptical if not dismissive executives from other auto companies who were overheard talking among themselves in front of the car later in the day.

But the journalists got it right with John Phillips from *Car & Driver* observing:

The car is significant no matter what becomes of it.

Clauspeter Becker of *Auto, Motor und Sport* wrote that:

Evoq's blend of design heritage and future has resulted in a daring, almost radical Cadillac. Evoq shows the guts to break the current mold.

Perhaps best of all, and a kind of tip of the hat to our targeted post-Boomer audience, was a letter I received several weeks later from a young car enthusiast in Oregon:

Dear Mr. Smith,

My name is Robbie Brooke. I'm seventeen years old. To-day I saw the cover of Car & Driver. Your car (Evoq) is one of the most beautiful autos I have ever seen. It possesses the same effortless beauty and elegance of a Ferrari 456 GT. It's so crisp, so refreshing, so aggressive. I want it just the way it is. For the sake of my future, please build the car I love!

Postscript

The public's enthusiasm for Evoq *did* result in a production program, to be built alongside the Corvette in GM's Bowling Green assembly plant. Unfortunately, the production car, XLR as it would be named, was about to lose its mojo due to a number of changes demanded by the vehicle line executive, his engineering leadership, and the manufacturing crew, mostly in the name of "common."

With little to lose, Cherry and I resolved to stand our ground. In the meeting to decide the styling and content of XLR, I laid out Cadillac's requirements, mostly the as-is Evoq, but with some compromises based on discussions to that point with the vehicle line executive. It was like lighting a fuse—with the bomb exploding when certain functional leaders sitting at the other end of the conference table, who controlled *all* the engineering and manufacturing resources, offered their opinions. "No" would be a very polite way of summarizing their thoughts. Cadillac's most expensive vehicle, certainly its flagship for some indefinite while, would be rounded down to "cheaper and easier to do." While it wasn't going to make or break Cadillac from a sales volume and profit point of view, it also wouldn't generate the gotta-have lust of Evoq. Wayne was so disappointed that he refused to sign the ceremonial program approval document at a subsequent Strategy Board meeting.

The XLR was introduced in 2003, and a little over 15,000 units were built before it was discontinued in 2009. While it does stand out somewhat on the road to this day, and V-Series versions with the supercharged Northstar are genuinely thrilling to drive, one is left to imagine what could have been had the original design of Robbie Brooke's dreams been retained. More investment would have been needed, but perhaps the full drama of Evoq would have produced higher annual volumes, a longer production run, and a more satisfying return on investment!

Figure 1 - 1st Gen Escalade

Figure 2 - 3rd Gen Escalade

Figure 3 - 1960 Eldorado - Copyright Parallel Productions/Tom Berthiaume (tom@faprops.com)

Figure 4 - Art & Science Form Vocabulary

Figure 5 - Art & Science Form Vocabulary

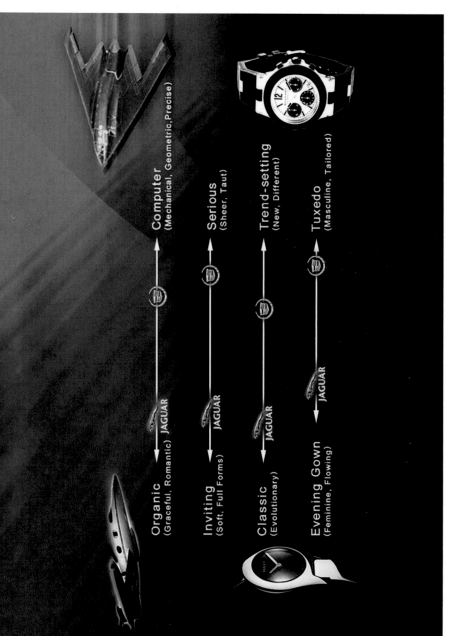

Figure 6 - Spectrum of Beauty

Figure 7 - Evoq Concept Car

Figure 8 - Imaj Concept Car

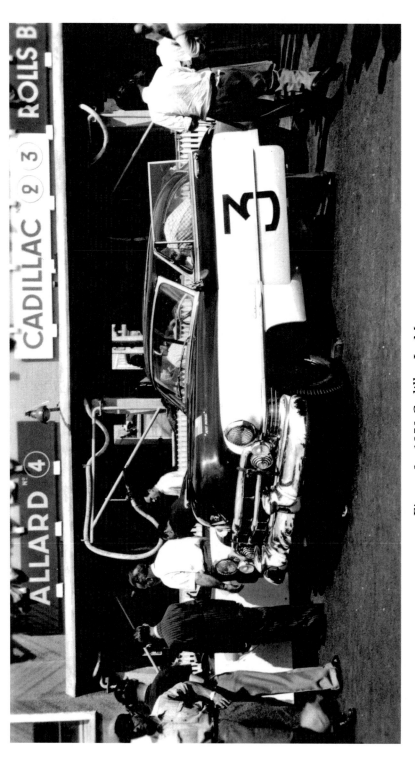

Figure 9 - 1950 Cadillac Le Mans race car

Figure 10 - 2000 Cadilac Le Mans race car

Figure 11 - 1996 Cadillac logo

Figure 12 - 1999 Cadillac logo

Figure 13 - 1997 Catera "Caddy That Zigs" spokesduck

Figure 14 - 1st Gen SRX (2004)

Figure 15 - 2003 CTS

Figure 16 - 2004 CTS-V

Figure 17 - 2005 STS-V

Figure 18 - 2008 CTS

Figure 19 - 2nd Gen SRX

Figure 20 - 2014 ELR

CHAPTER 5

BRANDAID

Evoq would be a road warrior for Cadillac over the next couple of years, appearing in auto shows all over the world—New York, Geneva, Dubai, Tokyo, and more. There would also be well-attended ride programs for our journalist friends—I mean, really, who wouldn't want to drive a supercharged NorthStar Cadillac two-seater with the top down? It was like that hyperspace moment that thrilled us all when seeing *Star Wars* for the first time!

These events generated considerable unpaid media for Cadillac, helping to raise the brand's profile, along with Escalade's introduction, of course. They would help build awareness and consideration for Cadillac in the run-up to the CTS introduction in 2002.

But we knew the brand would need more content, more news, *more* reasons to keep the media spotlight on a changing Cadillac. And we still had work to do on the rest of the brand's go-to-market elements—naming and logos, advertising, promotions, retail environments, processes, etc.—to make sure *all* things were lining up to look, smell, and feel like Art & Science before the CTS launch.

Night Vision

We managed to accomplish a lot with the media following Evoq, beginning with the launch of Night Vision a few months later. Part of Evoq's technology package, a production version of Night Vision was demonstrated on the Deville in a media event in Washington, DC. This was a first, featuring an infrared camera located in the center of the grille and a heads-up display projected on the lower windshield in front of the driver. The camera easily highlighted people or animals (think deer) along the roadside at night three to five times beyond the normal range of headlights.

Such safety-oriented technology was arguably territory most luxury consumers associated with Volvo. Cadillac's deployment of Night Vision seemed to challenge that overnight, earning the brand tons of media coverage, including above-the-fold, front page coverage in *USA Today*! It was a great technology message and allowed Cadillac's crack public relations team to draw the media back into the brand's long history of firsts, including many safety features. It was also spot on with the brand's embrace of leadership in *active* safety, one of the five product characteristics associated with the Art & Science positioning.

More Concept Cars

Additional concept cars were commissioned to hold the

public's attention. Concept cars were then developed by others, using centralized resources outside of Cadillac's control, but Wayne was still running design and was *quite* committed to Cadillac's new form. Most of these concept cars would foreshadow actual production models and wouldn't have the same pure and unadulterated concept purpose of Evoq.

The first of these was the Imaj, which was the forthcoming CTS sedan on steroids, disguised a bit but closer in styling to the actual CTS. Simon Cox, working out of his Birmingham, England, studio, led the design work on Imaj, which was introduced at the Geneva Motor Show in 2000. (Figure 8)

Car and Driver's Frank Markus referred to Imaj as *"Lesson No. 2 in 'How to Speak Cadillac.'"* Chalk that up as a win!

Imaj was followed by Vizon, introduced at NAIAS in 2001. Vizon was meant to telegraph Cadillac's forthcom-

Almost everyone started at "No" or "Are you kidding?" but gradually worked their way to neutral. At that point, our quest morphed into some version of dominoes, looking for that first agreeable stakeholder and enlisting their support to help persuade others who had a vote. Phil Guarascio, GM's global marketing leader and a close confidant of Ron Zarrella's, and John Middlebrook (my new boss and GM's acknowledged racing guru) were super-helpful in this regard. By early 1999, we were finally good to go.

Riley & Scott Cars would get the assignment to develop the bespoke race cars, which would be powered by twin-turbocharged Northstar engines producing 650 horsepower. Kip Wasenko was assigned to drive as much of Cadillac's design language into the car as high-speed racing aerodynamics would allow—and it was a beauty! (Figure 10)

We had few illusions of actually winning at Le Mans, having had zero racing experience in the intervening five decades, but we certainly would put our best foot forward. In any event, as Marshall McLuhan observed, "The *medium* is (was) the message."

With an approved program and work on the race cars underway, we announced our return to Le Mans at a small dinner for journalists during the Geneva Motor Show in March 1999. A quarter-scale model of the work-in-process race car had been prepared and was sitting, draped, among the high-top cocktail tables in our private dining room.

When the car was unveiled, there was a moment of silence—then a bunch of "Holy-cow!"-type reactions from the group. Having soaked in bits and pieces of Art & Science since Pebble Beach the prior August, followed by Evoq's introduction in January, the guests didn't need any help connecting the dots. Cadillac racing made every bit as much sense to them as it did to us, and they were excited.

A future GM employee (and a future boss) was also

geeked at the announcement. Back in Detroit at a fund-raising dinner, Bob Lutz cornered me and said the move was GM's best decision in years! Of course, Bob had an unquenchable and well-documented need for speed, in all forms!

To be fair, our first year on the track wasn't great. Cadillac's two prototypes finished the race in thirteenth and fourteenth places, but the media coverage before, during, and after the race made the investment hugely successful in terms of awareness of the changing Cadillac. Cadillac's participation in Le Mans was limited to the three years between 2000 and 2002. But it served its purpose in stoking media interest prior to the CTS introduction.

And the CTS would prove to be a way better platform to demonstrate Cadillac's performance bona fides anyway!

In 2004, Cadillac would enter the SCCA World Challenge GT circuit with a track-ready CTS-VR, which socked away ten wins and dozens of podium finishes in just a few years—along the way, overcoming occasional rule changes intended to, um, level the playing field. SCCA racing legitimized the introduction of the first-ever, *street*-ready, 400 horsepower CTS-V later in 2004, the first in what would be a long and distinguished line of Cadillac performance variants known as the V-Series.

Addressing the (Fussy) Logo

Setting the hardware aside—concept cars, race cars, and the future product portfolio were all in hand—the software of Cadillac was being rewritten. Product names, brand marques, the look and feel of our dealerships, and more was subject to change. Everything needed to be consistently rendered as if from the same bolt of Art & Science cloth.

We started with Cadillac's brand marque, the venerable

wreath and crest. Changing logos is not for the faint at heart since brands risk losing the visual identity they've invested years (and money) in cultivating, and a *new* investment is required to change everything from business cards to dealer signage. It all adds up. Still, in the context of Art & Science, the current logo—in place for thirty-five years and changed minimally along the way—seemed dated.

By 1998, Cadillac had had seven designs over its 100-year history—more like thirty if minor refinements along the way were also included. The marque had evolved over time, but it had retained certain distinctive and recognizable elements, notably the Mondrian-inspired crest, with its prominent use of red and gold, with black, silver, and blue highlights. The proportions of the crest might change, as might the placement and execution of the wreath and other details, but it was easy to see the different versions over time respected Cadillac's history and pedigree.

The 1998 version placed the crest within the wreath, with small pearls across the top of the crest, and with merlettes (birds of a sort) located in the Mondrian field. (Figure 11)

When we showed luxury customers this logo in the context of either Evoq or the Art & Science design language, they overwhelmingly embraced a new logo design which was cleaner, sleeker, and more youthful—even incorporating some added relief (depth on the z-axis) as if to communicate the same faceting and angles of the new Cadillac design language. (Figure 12)

While the team (Cadillac and Design) quickly aligned on a new brand logo, some lingering disagreement existed over the Cadillac script. Research here was inconclusive, but the Cadillac script was truly lovely and recognizable from a mile away, even if one was squinting. Wayne Cherry and I went with our gut, choosing to retain the script and never looked back.

Cadillac, What Art Thy Name(s)?

Product naming nomenclature was another area of research, and debate. In 1998, Cadillac was Seville, Deville, El Dorado, and Catera, and most of these names were well established in the luxury market. Cadillac's competition, save Lincoln, had been using alphanumeric model names for years without much, if any, media criticism or consumer complaint. Would retaining the current names be consistent with Art & Science? If we attempted to retain the established names, would we risk losing some control of positioning the new vehicles because some in the media would inevitably compare and contrast old and new Cateras, Sevilles, etc.? And were such comparisons in our interest?

We believed a naming convention change was in order, so we tested various alternatives with luxury vehicle owners and Millennial and Gen Xer future buyers. We considered what Cadillac's competitors had done, but we found, in some cases, their embedded engine displacement and/or European segment designators to be unworkable for Cadillac. And we did *not* want to copy their nomenclature exactly. Ultimately, we chose to use three letters, and for sedans the last two letters would be TS (for touring sedan). The first letter would be taken from the current model: C from Catera, S from Seville, and D from Deville, so CTS, STS, and DTS. The CTS crossover would be named SRX, with the X denoting crossover, and the Evoq-inspired two-seater would be named XLR, where the LR denoted luxury. Because 'Slade was becoming a cross-generational rock star, we left the name alone.

Cadillac's Everyday Face—Dealer Showrooms

Luxury vehicle dealerships are a vital part of the customer experience, no less so than how other luxury goods (e.g., apparel, watches, etc.) are presented and sold. Luxury vehicles are expensive products, bought by men and women accustomed to high levels of attention and service. The dealership locations, their exteriors, their interiors, and the bearing and competence of the sales and service personnel all leave an impression, and those are expected to be uniformly good impressions, almost extensions of a luxury customer's sense of self. Think "accomplished, successful, discriminating."

Whereas Mercedes, BMW, and Lexus might have 300-400 dealers across the United States, in 1998, Cadillac had around *1,600 locations*! Only 150 or so sold *only* Cadillacs, but they accounted for 50 percent of Cadillac's annual sales. The remaining Cadillac franchises were located in smaller urban, suburban, and rural areas, and were sold in facilities alongside anywhere from one to four other GM brands. Cadillac wasn't core business for these dealers, so it seldom got its due in terms of a given dealership's upscale look and feel, or enough sales training to persuasively present Cadillac models compared to competitive makes.

For all Cadillac dealers, big or small, the steady decline in Cadillac's fortunes and its uncertain future left many stores in need of upgrades and some stores in need of new, higher-traffic locations. For all of Cadillac's decades of success, many of its locations had been left high and dry by outward growth in many communities. Later-to-arrive luxury competitors had some advantages in building stores in new suburbia. (BMW opened its first US dealership in 1975.) Visually, the range of curbside images for Cadillac covered a lot of ground, most of it not good.

In May 1998 we hosted about 100 of Cadillac's best dealers at the annual Cadillac Master Dealer Conference in Naples. The year before, we had told this group we were in the process of reimagining the brand. This time we could share the details of Art & Science with them—important-

ly, including a broad sketch of related new product intro-
ductions.

Like most business meetings, mornings were devoted to
classroom-style business updates, and afternoons were
given over to team building, fun, and socializing. The deep
dive into Art & Science would take place the morning of
day one. We went through a lot of the same detail and ra-
tionale that had been shared with the Strategy Board a few
months before. It was important to do so because these
dealers, when they returned home, would share the key
points with other Cadillac dealers in their regions. (Cadillac dealers typically cooperated in advertising in local
markets.) They would hopefully be excited and enthusiastic in doing so, delivering yet another installment of hope
in the process.

You could hear a pin drop during the presentation.

And when the time came for the morning session to adjourn, with some dealers antsy to make a mad dash for the doors to get ready for their afternoon activities, we still had their full attention for the additional ten to fifteen minutes needed to finish up.

This was an especially important moment of "Brandaid" since these dealers, our most experienced, highest volume, and best capitalized dealers, were genuinely excited about the potential for their Cadillac franchises. They felt the factory's commitment to the brand and understood that reaching its full potential would also require investment on their part. And their actions would pull many other Cadillac dealers along.

Carl Sewell would write to Jack Smith after the Master Dealer event, saying,

> I want to let you know how encouraged I was by Cadillac's New Vision. It is the first time in my recollection that we have had a plan to win at Cadillac.

Mark Hennesy, chairman of Cadillac's dealer council at the time, noted in a later *Automotive News* article,

> *We've seen the future, and the future is ours. For once, going forward for the next six years, Cadillac dealers have a lot to look forward to.*

Escalade was Hope 1.0…getting Cadillac into the fast-growing luxury SUV business, helping to retain Cadillac owners, and creating new revenue and profits for both dealers and GM alike. Art & Science was Hope 2.0, a detailed plan to transform the brand and its entire product portfolio and to credibly attract new generations of luxury consumers. Cadillac was attractive and investable again for dealers and, as a result, the market value of Cadillac franchises would rise markedly over the next few years.

You Need Professional Help!

Investment on the dealers' part would take the form of

reimaging their facilities and, for some (especially where Cadillac was in the same facility as other GM brands), significant reengineering of sales and service practices. A starting point for this work was bringing in Wolf Olins to prepare a Cadillac brand book, which would illustrate the brand logos, color palate, and material textures of Art & Science. The book was developed in close cooperation with Design and informed, obviously, by Cadillac's new form vocabulary and century-old embrace of the Mondrian crest. Once developed, the brand book was used to guide the look and feel of everything, everywhere—office decor, dealership reimaging, the Cadillac studio in GM's design center, Cadillac displays and promotional materials, owner's manuals, product catalogues, communications materials, brand-themed gifts, stationary, advertising, business cards, etc.

With the brand book in hand, Cadillac engaged Andre Putnam and, later, Booziotis and Experience Engineering to develop a reimaging plan for Cadillac dealerships. Automotive dealers know a *lot* about facility-related costs, and the handful of Cadillac dealers who were asked to be part of this work had each undertaken a number of building and remodeling projects over the years, for both the GM and competitive franchises they owned. Getting their input and buy-in would clearly help in developing a program that most, if not all, dealers could support. GM also had an experienced dealer facility group that participated in this effort, which was especially important since most Cadillac retail locations were showrooms shared with other GM brands.

The results of the effort were greatly improved showrooms for Cadillac's new product—modern, clean, and upscale, sporting the colors of Art & Science.

At times, the four-year wait for CTS seemed more like forty, but it provided time to thoughtfully rewire Cadillac's go-to-market strategies. It also required the Cadillac team and select parts of the larger GM team to plumb the depths of their collective creativity to create a stream of relevant news about a changing Cadillac—and they came through big time!

CHAPTER 6

FRIENDLY FIRE

The story of Cadillac's turnaround has, up to this point, been presented largely in chronological order. Along the way, however, there were scuffles with colleagues and functional staffs about executing various aspects of the Art & Science plan. These conflicts were certainly distracting and time consuming, and not all overcome despite presumably working from an approved strategy.

What I can say is that leading a turnaround is a whole lot easier when you're on top and control all the levers of change. That was my experience at Allison Transmission, which immediately preceded my work at Cadillac. Allison is located in Indianapolis, some 300 miles from Detroit. Apart from the insulating distance, Allison was not part of GM's core vehicle operations and was fully equipped with its own engineering, purchasing, and manufacturing resources. While capital was needed from time to time, there were no mothership functional groups to consult or corporate approval processes to make one's way through. During my three years at Allison, I would simply call my boss, either Bill Hoglund or Harry Pearce, explain our proposal, and receive approval in short order. It certainly helped that Jack Smith visited Allison several times, where forthcoming investment proposals could be previewed.

Once, when talking with someone who worked for Pearce, I noted that Harry was great to work with and very responsive to my requests, but he never *initiated* contact. The reply spoke volumes: "Harry only calls when there's a problem," which sounded like, "You're in charge and expected to get results. If you can't, we'll find someone who can."

It was different at Cadillac. I might be responsible, but I had little authority to act. In fact, by this time in GM's history, marketing divisions only controlled sales and marketing, and even these activities would be further ring-fenced starting in 1999 courtesy of the FMIT study.

All resources related to the brand's *products* were in the hands of the engineering, manufacturing, planning, and purchasing leaders who sat on the North American Strategy Board. My boss, Ron Zarrella, was also on this board, and was responsible for vehicle marketing, sales, and service...for *eight* brands. And Cadillac wasn't the volume/market share/profitability engine of the North American business. That honor fell to Chevrolet and GMC, home to full-size pickups and SUVS, which paid *all* the bills.

The bruising battle to land Escalade in my first year was a kind of canary in the coal mine, presaging the many subsequent firefights over nearly every change at Cadillac. The

Art & Science strategy received important and substantial financial support for *most*, but not all, of its component parts. Various executives second-guessed CTS right up to its introduction, receding into the shadows when it was a success. Still others nearly put the kibosh on the first generation SRX, Cadillac's top-selling model today.

The opportunity for Cadillac in Europe and other global markets was effectively killed by regional leaders setting the brand up for failure with misguided and underfunded marketing and distribution plans, and powertrain leaders who wanted little if anything to do with the gasoline and diesel engines needed for export markets. Still others proposed wholly different luxury strategies for GM, and not so long after Art & Science was approved.

Some opportunity for Cadillac was certainly lost to the energy expended to fend off such friendly fire. Changed market or competitive conditions are a fact of life and can force unwelcome and costly strategy changes, and "Suck it up, buttercup" applies in such circumstances. But executing Art & Science exposed fault lines in GM's operating culture in the late 1990s and early 2000s, no doubt the result of waves of well-intentioned organizational and process change. GM's matrix organization. . .regions on one side, functions on the other. . .was a most complicated delivery system for Cadillac's global Art & Science strategy, and there would be costly omissions as a result.

Brand Management

GM's deteriorating financial performance and thirty-year market share slide was covered previously and, as noted, by 1992 the company's board had had enough. Jack Smith became the new CEO and presided over a complete overhaul of the company. That would include the "customer" side of the business, for which Ron Zarrella was hired away from Bausch & Lomb in 1994 to become the GM North America vice president of sales and marketing.

Ron brought with him, and installed, the concept of brand management, and brand manager positions and supporting teams were created for every *model* (e.g., Impala, Yukon, and Deville). Talent for the brand manager positions came from both within and outside of GM, with the outsiders having served in similar positions at package goods companies like Procter & Gamble.

To be fair, this new and very significant focus on the consumer was desperately needed and produced, in time, some worthy and durable positioning of our brands, which were otherwise suffering from an identity crisis. "Professional Grade," for example, was developed to further differentiate Chevrolet from GMC trucks and SUVs, with GMC owners seeing themselves and their vehicles as up-market from their Chevrolet siblings.

A downside to brand management at GM was that the brand managers were, as noted, *model*-based and quite often indifferent (sometimes even hostile) to the needs of the mothership, i.e., Chevrolet or, in my case, Cadillac.

For example, when I arrived at Cadillac in early 1997, the new Catera was about to launch. This vehicle would enter the highest-volume luxury segment in the United States, so-called entry luxury, where the likes of the Mercedes's C-Class and the BMW 3 played and played hard. Cadillac was certainly late to this party, and its last attempt to offer a small luxury experience, the Cimarron, had met with considerable ridicule. The Catera was a competent rear-wheel-drive vehicle known as the Opel Omega in Europe. The Omega was "new" in 1994, meaning its styling was locked down sometime in 1991. To this dated look, only some minor refinements could be made, along with Cadillac-related jewelry.

The Catera brand management team, with support from Cadillac's ad agency, had landed on the tagline, "The Caddy That Zigs!" and enlisted a red, cartoon duck as the product's spokesperson (Figure 13)

Oh, man....

Since luxury vehicle buyers are a serious sort, I was sure few if any consumers would be moved by a cartoon duck to put Catera on their shopping lists alongside the C-Class and 3-Series. But the brand manager was among the first of his peers to launch a vehicle under the new brand management orthodoxy and was, as a result, getting *lots* of help and coaching from those above—from above me, that is. As we hadn't yet started the reimaging work for Cadillac, there was no unique endgame for all Cadillac models to be a part of, including Catera. With the launch upon us, the red duck would be leading the charge.

All Cadillac brand managers had this early-days "independence" streak, inculcated by their model-based brand management training. To a person, and given Cadillac's poor image at the time, the brand managers sought minimal association with the venerable wreath and crest. In fact, as planning for the next-gen Seville ramped up in mid-1997, its brand manager literally wanted nothing to do with Cadillac.

The best I could do on arrival in 1997 was to offer a kind of reality check, which went something like this: "Folks, today GM doesn't budget enough money for each of its eight marketing divisions to have competitive awareness. It most certainly won't have enough money for each of its sixty-plus model-level brands to get anywhere close! The only hope for your brands is that Cadillac gets hot again. And, by the way, in the luxury space, luxury vehicle owners most often respond, when asked what they're driving, that they're driving a Benz or a Bimmer."

As we began to wrap up the Art & Science work by the end of 1997, the friction loss experienced early on with the brand managers gave way to an enthusiastic embrace of what it could mean for the styling, ride, handling, and technology of their respective products. Collectively, we agreed that the values of the newly reimaged Cadillac would be an exciting and reassuring foundation for all models in their respective go-to-market messaging.

Needless to say, this hard-won consensus on rallying around Cadillac to promote all of the brand's models didn't go over so well with Ron. A fair number of arguments followed, and our relationship predictably soured some more. At one point, I believe Ron even described my thinking as "narrow." However, after a few months, and with the help of very senior ad agency executives and Phil Guarascio, Ron relented and allowed us the needed latitude within brand management to focus on Cadillac and, ultimately, Art & Science in our messaging.

The red duck was never heard from again.

Kwan

As noted earlier, in late 1997, Ron launched a study of possible centralization of various and otherwise independent sales and marketing activities of the car divisions. This was the Field Management Integration Team (FMIT). Duplicate back-office activities like order intake and distribution, promotions, dealer development, motor sports, special vehicles (including concept cars), and others would be centralized to eliminate overlap, reduce overhead, and improve purchasing practices. The divisions would continue to have a voice in all these things, but final decisions would reside elsewhere in the newly enlarged VSSM (Vehicle Sales, Service, and Marketing) headquarters operation. Everyone could imagine the inevitability of queuing up for a smaller pie over time, probably slower response times as well, and even arguments as to what the required divisional "finish" on this or that really needed to be. Still, from a GM perspective, there *was* clear overlap and opportunity in the back-office and the divisional general managers could only hope that the newly centralized operations, staffed as they would be from those with divisional experience, would be as professional and accommodating as they were used to.

The bigger idea in the FMIT study was the consolidation of the divisional field sales teams into a single entity, leaving the marketing divisions with just that, marketing responsibilities, including brand management and advertising. The only exception would be Saturn—that standalone, do-it-all-different car division would be left alone. The FMIT study team, aided by Mars & Co, stated that the:

Full promise of brand management is impeded by the legacy sales organization...and that a single sales force...

will also give GM more influence with its dealers.

It's still hard to believe those words were written with a straight face, and I suspect it was more what someone wanted to hear than what the study team itself believed. Brand management had issues, yes, but none due to the divisional field sales forces. As for influence with dealers, while those selling multiple GM brands would no doubt appreciate streamlined contacts from the factory that consolidation would bring, influence derives from hot products that dealers are keen to get more than their fair share of. Period.

In any event, it was hard to be objective about losing control of your sales force, and I wasn't alone. All the marketing division general managers were concerned with this possibility, believing the brands would suffer if the direct link between themselves and their dealers was severed and replaced by a third-party managed by others, and having different performance metrics and different loyalties.

This area of concern, qualitative as it was, came to be known as the Kwan, the spirit binding together everyone associated with a brand from divisional HQ to the dealer showrooms, informing all of their work, every day. Sales force consolidation was seen as a threat to shared pride and brand-based calls to action, ultimately to the detriment of sales and profits. The FMIT study team didn't officially share this concern, but I don't think their hearts were in the argument since they all grew up in one marketing division or another. And, to be fair, they had been given the "answer" at the *beginning* of their study!

Some might be wondering what, if anything, does all of this back-office reorganization mean for the retail customer—the target of Cadillac's Art & Science repositioning? It doesn't affect their experience, right? Does it really matter?

I thought it did, and still do.

No other luxury competitor employed a contract sales force, a fact *not* lost on some of Cadillac's best dealers who also sold luxury competitive makes. Many Cadillac dealers were upset with the sales force consolidation once it was announced, finding it impossible to square with the Art & Science vision. Many dealers wrote letters to GM's senior leaders, pleading for Cadillac to retain its sales force, but "common"-related momentum in GM at the time was a near-impossible force to resist, let alone overcome. The pleadings fell on deaf ears, and the NADA dealer survey published in November 1998 gave voice to Cadillac dealers' renewed displeasure—despite Escalade and the promise of Art & Science, the brand had *dropped* to second from the bottom!

Setting aside the issue of control, there were also concerns about before/after talent working with Cadillac's dealers.

We had some of the best field sales personnel in GM, perhaps across the industry, largely due to some terrific recruiting, training, and mentoring that most of the field sales force had received from Cadillac's long-time general sales manager, Pete Gerosa. Cadillac also had unique dealer-facing incentive and recognition programs, which the brand's sales force understood and used to good effect. This was all at risk, and the consolidation offered no convincing solutions.

The much bigger talent problem was that FMIT proposed to address GM's dealers with five-person teams (market area manager, sales, service, parts, finance, and insurance) that would call on *all* GM dealers in a given area, not just Chevrolet, not just Cadillac, but *all*.

These teams would need a decent understanding of *all* of GM's sixty-plus models—content, unique or class-leading features, pricing and incentives, competitive models, etc. They would need to understand *all* facility imaging requirements, *all* local dealer advertising programs, *all* divisional recognition programs, etc. In effect, FMIT would take field sales personnel who had solid subject matter command of one division (not acquired overnight, by the way) and personal relationships with the dealers they served, and multiply their required content mastery *by seven*, further leavened with a host of *new* team and dealer relationships to build at the same time.

Crazy.

It was impossible scope, no matter how smart, energetic, and well-intentioned the field sales cadre was. And it was going to be really bad for Cadillac and its dealers because these new teams would be subject to a new, *volume-based* incentive compensation scheme. It would become second nature for the teams responding either to sales pressure from above or motivated by the sales commission opportunity to focus on higher-volume Chevrolet and GMC brands, at Cadillac's (and GM's) expense.

On several occasions, I made the case for keeping Cadillac intact and out of the FMIT consolidation. Heck, if an exception was being made for Saturn, surely, we could talk about doing the same with Cadillac. Otherwise, we would be unique among luxury marques in *not* having a dedicated sales organization, and there was no reason to believe GM had some secret sauce in this regard. We offered to reorganize our teams to mirror the FMIT organizational form and offer nearly the same overhead savings. More importantly, I firmly believed that any foregone cost savings would be repaid many times over in terms of higher volumes and profit for Cadillac and for GM.

On this latter point, GM in Canada had been operating in that much smaller market with a single sales force servicing all brands for years, and Cadillac's share of the Canadian luxury market was 400 basis points *lower* compared to the US. A share decline of that magnitude in the United States was about 50,000 fewer sales and a net income hit of $300 million.

I would have expected to hear "stop the presses."

Instead, I was told GM Canada's president "didn't share my viewpoint"…with no rebuttal to either the market share data or the related profit hit. My argument simply fell on deaf ears, all things "common" won another round, and Cadillac lost control of its sales force on January 1, 1999.

Implementation of the FMIT consolidation encountered rough waters from the outset because the new order intake and distribution system (aka VOMS) was *not* ready for prime time. This truth had been put on the table in the Fall of 1998 by Bob Coletta, the journeyman Buick general manager who piloted VOMS in his division during the second half of 1998. Coletta advised Ron and the FMIT team that the new system was too difficult for dealers to use to configure orders, and it was also proving troublesome in invoicing dealers for vehicles shipped to them from GM assembly plants. In other words, GM's order flow and revenue from its dealers was at risk.

Notwithstanding this advice, Zarrella held fast to the original FMIT launch date of January 1, 1999. Almost immediately, *all* GM dealers experienced problems with trying to order vehicles, and GM, in turn, experienced problems invoicing dealers. VOMS' launch was a disaster...an avoidable one for sure...and followed by several months of very labor-intensive workarounds until system glitches could be addressed.

In subsequent years, certain other aspects of the FMIT reorganization design gave way to reality—the five-person dealer contact teams were reconstituted to obtain more exclusive focus for specific divisional brands, which represented a return to a more manageable scope *and* improved service levels to the dealers. Also, the volume-based incentive scheme was abandoned altogether, partly due to its complicated workings and partly due to a market-share-at-all-costs behavior that the company was slowly beginning to wean itself from.

Global Luxury Group

Shortly after the North American Strategy Board had approved the Art & Science strategy, Bob Hendry, who was then the managing director of Saab, sent a detailed note to GM's senior leadership proposing the formation of a Global Luxury Group made up of Cadillac and Saab. There was good analysis of the global luxury market, GM's checkered history in that segment, suggestions about positioning GM's two brands in a complementary way, and thoughts about acquiring or partnering with a third luxury brand to build out a more compelling portfolio. (GM would, in fact, explore such possibilities with both Alfa Romeo and BMW over the next year or so.)

Hendry recommended this new group be co-managed by GM's two presidents at the time, Rick Wagoner managing the Americas and Lou Hughes managing everything else (including Europe, where Saab was based). Hendry, Larry Burns from Planning, and I would round out the group.

The proposal included ideas about the attractive economics of a coordinated approach, most notably in the area of platform sharing and related savings. Very specifically, Bob recommended that Cadillac and Saab share front-wheel drive architectures, which was what Saab had always used. There were also comments about luxury buyers styling preferences, noting that GM entries should "comply with European criteria for efficiency and understatement." To support understatement, research was cited suggesting that only 35 percent of luxury buyers indicated "design" as a principal reason for purchase.

Sigh.

It had been only two weeks since the Strategy Board reviewed and approved Art & Science, a strategy that expressly embraced a return to bold design and *rear-wheel-drive* architecture. Cadillac had tried understatement and gone to the limit of front-wheel-drive capabilities, coming up short on both counts compared to the luxury market leaders. One could understand Saab's embrace of these characteristics since it was in their Scandinavian genes and, with them, they had cultivated over time a unique, almost cultish and *very* loyal following.

The proposal for Cadillac and Saab to share front-wheel-drive architectures actually seemed a bit desperate and most likely a statement of sorts that Saab was *not* getting what it needed from architecture sharing with Opel (such sharing was among the principal reasons for GM acquiring Saab in 1990). Opel products were developed for high volume and would clearly offer greater scale to Saab than any Cadillac-Saab combination could. That said, Saab did have difficulty at times obtaining engineering changes related to either up-market refinements and/or features they wished to offer their tonier and more discriminating customers, hence, the notion of throwing in with Cadillac.

Bob Hendry was unaware of the Strategy Board's action on Cadillac and not happy when he learned about what Art & Science meant. He was critical of the decision, taken in isolation from Saab, and openly doubted the rear-wheel-drive choice "would be executed in a competitive manner." For several months thereafter, planning attempted to explore GM's global luxury strategy options—at one point even suggesting that a "harvest Cadillac" option be considered.

Wait! What? Had planning not been in the Strategy Board meeting not so many months before?

For a time, Hendry's proposal consumed time and resources, but it went nowhere. By August, he stated flatly that he would no longer participate in any global luxury strategy work and would devote all of his energies to Saab and Saab alone. He did see opportunity in Cadillac and Saab sharing distribution globally, as I did. Other parts of GM, notably the regional presidents, did *not*, and that promising bit of luxury cooperation suffered an early death.

Ten years later, and as a by-product of its bankruptcy, GM sold Saab.

Oldsillac

By the summer of 1999, the FMIT consolidations had

been in place for months. Every marketing division, skinnied down as they were, had new general managers. Given the in-process turnaround at Cadillac, I was asked to stay on, and I was reporting to John Middlebrook, the first vice president of marketing in the reorganized VSSM organization. Middlebrook and I had met fifteen years earlier when we had both worked at Pontiac. He had great experience in both marketing and sales, at Pontiac and later at Chevrolet, and was one of the most open and candid GM leaders I have ever worked with.

One day in his office, Middlebrook handed me a copy of a note that was circulating about strategic options for Oldsmobile. I wasn't on the distribution list but Middlebrook had always been an inclusive operator. The note explored a range of options, but the preferred option was the merger of Cadillac and Oldsmobile. It had been prepared by the Oldsmobile team, then led by Karen Francis. Karen was one of the original brand managers recruited by Ron

Zarrella into GM from another packaged goods firm at the time brand management was launched in 1995. With the FMIT reorganization, she became the general manager of Oldsmobile.

Like nearly all GM divisions, Oldsmobile's sales had taken a hit. In 1994, the brand sold nearly 470,000 vehicles but, by 1997, that number had fallen to just shy of 300,000. The new Alero compact improved sales to 311,000 in 1998 and to 378,000 in 1999, but that would be as good as it would ever get. The handwriting had been on the wall for some time since Oldsmobile was getting squeezed from both within and without. For all its good intentions, BrandScape couldn't defy gravity and create a sustainable position for Oldsmobile, flanked as it was by Chevy below and Buick above. The endless tide of really good, mid-size competitive makes further ate into Oldsmobile's reason for being. All-in profit analysis would show that the brand was at best a break-even proposition for GM and heading south. That said, given the bite of state-based dealer franchise laws, closing Oldsmobile would be quite expensive.

The principal argument for the merger proposal was that Olds was already having some success attracting the younger buyers Cadillac was seeking with Art & Science. The proposal also suggested increasing the number of Cadillac-Oldsmobile dealers from 200 to 350, such that this channel would handle nearly half of Cadillac's sales.

I was certain there wasn't any secret sauce in Olds' marketing and that the right product and the right marketing would increase Cadillac's appeal to younger buyers. We were already seeing this with Escalade. I was also quite certain that increasing Cadillac's dealer count was just plain dumb—we had 1,600 locations already, four times those of Mercedes, BMW, or Lexus.

The merger proposal no doubt arose out of Oldsmobile's desperate and darkening future, but there was little value in it for GM. Consolidation synergies would be few—pretty much limited to some headcount reductions in the crews reporting directly to the two general managers. The big-ticket items—product lines, dealerships, advertising, and promotions—wouldn't change. One thing that *might* change, however, was how the combined entity would respond to the everyday pressure for sales volume and market share. Like the FMIT teams' likely behavior, the merged entity, responding to top line pressures from above, would likely bias the combined advertising and incentive dollars under its control to the lower-priced Oldsmobile models.

This would not be good for Cadillac and its dealers, or GM for that matter.

After a few hours' reflection, I shared my thoughts with Middlebrook. For several weeks thereafter, the circulating "Oldsillac" proposal prompted a flurry of email, notes, and meetings, but it got no traction. Three years later, GM would close Oldsmobile for good.

"Cadillac Common," Nixed

For all of the effort GM put into leaning out its structure and implementing standardized work in the product development process, competitive product quality remained elusive. Third party comparisons would show GM consistently lagging behind almost everyone else, save the other domestic manufacturers. Japanese makes had cornered the market on quality and were often the first reason consumers offered up for buying the likes of Toyota and Nissan.

As GM lagged in the quality arena, so did Cadillac. Despite top management calls for improvement, the needle hardly moved on Cadillac during most of the '90s—no surprise, really, since Cadillac did not control any of the engineering, purchasing, or manufacturing ingredients that determined the outcome.

But neither did the leaders of Lexus or Infiniti, and yet

their quality was top of the charts and meaningfully better than their high-scoring Toyota and Nissan siblings. How does that happen?

Because they do *different* "common" things for their luxury offerings.

I know this because I asked A. T. Kearney shortly after my arrival at Cadillac to identify any differences in the product development processes at Toyota and Nissan that might account for the higher quality scores of their luxury offerings.

By July, the results were in. Both companies had dedicated vehicle development centers for luxury cars, with both more employees (to some extent, reflecting more content) and less turnover. Both companies employed a longer vehicle development timeline, anywhere from three to eight months longer, all of which was spent in the all-important prototype phase, where performance and fit-and-finish is perfected. The longer prototype phase employed additional and more sophisticated evaluation methods and provided time for longer die development and assembly plant preparation that takes place in parallel.

Both companies built luxury vehicles on dedicated assembly lines that typically ran 50 percent *slower* than those building Corollas. Here again, some but not all of this extra time could be explained by the more complex, feature-rich luxury models. While neither company, *per se*, approached supplier selection differently, it was evident from interviews that suppliers were expected to put their best personnel on luxury components, doing more design iterations, and employing their best technology. Successful suppliers would enjoy higher margins, albeit on lower sales volumes.

One could imagine that such documented additional care and feeding would produce better results. Certainly, if the industry's leading practitioners of "lean" and "common" reasoned their way to *two* common systems, so could GM. So, we shared these insights and proposed that a small engineering and manufacturing team close ranks with Cadillac and A.T. Kearney to determine what similar accommodations might be possible in the development of future Cadillac models.

Sadly, there was no appetite for "Cadillac Common," notwithstanding the rock-solid benchmarking work. GM was busy perfecting and institutionalizing its *single* product development system, and erecting a second one for Cadillac was apparently too much to contemplate. That said, I recall Jack Smith, who made "run lean and run common" an important if not bankruptcy-avoiding organizational mantra in the early '90s, later observing that he wished he had added "when it makes sense."

Underpowered

Art & Science laid out a portfolio of luxury models that
provided solid market coverage in North America and decent coverage for Europe and other export markets (lack-
ing only a luxury offering below the Catera/CTS). The
right powertrain options figured importantly in all of this.

In the US, all Cadillacs except Catera were equipped with
gasoline V-8 engines; customer competitive analysis made
it clear that V-6 engines were needed across the portfolio.
For our global ambitions, we had to take Europe's engine
displacement-based taxes into account, which clearly in-
centivized smaller, 4-cylinder engines, and we also needed to offer a diesel as well since they accounted for nearly 40 percent of all vehicle sales. Importantly, we would
need all-wheel-drive options to support the Art & Science
promise of all-weather control, to be sure, but also because of growing consumer demand for this capability in
passenger cars.

These requirements proved *quite* difficult to secure.

We had to twist a lot of arms on the notion of offering V-6 engines in the 2003 SRX and 2005 STS, even though the segment-leading Lexus RS was 100 percent V-6, and Mercedes and BMW were already offering V-6s in the premium luxury segment where the STS would play (in some cases, also flanked by four- and eight-cylinder options). While it does represent added engineering and manufacturing work to package each additional family of engines in a given vehicle, it also expands market coverage, sales, and profits.

The idea that we needed a V-6 was accepted, but the struggle was far from over. In August 1999, GM's powertrain group proposed a V-6 for SRX in 2005, two years *after* its introduction, *no* diesel engine, ever, and *no* AWD for Seville, ever.

So much for Powertrain's support for Art & Science!

Months of back-and-forth ensued; watching sausage getting made would have been more satisfying. The good news was we had V-6 engines available *at launch* for both SRX and STS, giving both models maximum market coverage.

The bad news was GM totally failed on a diesel engine, which was especially important for the CTS in Europe, and it wasn't for the lack of good options. Two turbo-charged, four-cylinder options were available—one internal (Opel) and one external (VM Motori)—and both compared nicely to four-cylinder diesel options found in the target competitors such as Mercedes C-Class and BMW 3-Series. Neither engine option was chosen—and for reasons having *nothing* to do with the customer. Despite prior Strategy Board agreement that Cadillac would be responsible for positioning its products across all markets, GM's European leadership decided CTS would compete in Europe against the larger Mercedes E-Class and BMW's 5 Series entries, where V-6 diesels were featured.

If all that CTS could offer was a four-cylinder diesel, they would pass on that engine option and pass on selling the car entirely.

@#$%&!

We can't know if, today, Cadillac would be enjoying a larger presence in Europe had GM proceeded with a four-cylinder diesel for the CTS, but my answer to that question would be yes. The higher sales volumes resulting from a diesel option in the CTS would have raised Cadillac's profile among European luxury consumers. More investment in models tailored to this market and better distribution could have followed, leading to even more sales. All of this potential was stymied by a GM Europe leadership team that took decisions rightfully belonging to Cadillac.

No LAVing Matter!

Cadillac's most successful model today, the SRX, came very close to never being born.

The new rear-wheel-drive architecture being developed for the CTS (aka, Sigma) was envisioned to support not only a larger STS sedan to replace the front-wheel-drive Seville but also a crossover vehicle, called LAV at the time. The sales leader in the luxury crossover market back then was the Lexus RS, but other car companies were getting into this growing segment. Luxury crossovers, like luxury SUVs, were the cat's meow then and now.

In scoping out the Cadillac LAV, a self-storing third row was initially seen as a category first and a competitive advantage. Early illustrations from design, trading on the Art & Science form vocabulary, suggested sleek, fast-back styling. All of this played well internally since nearly every automobile manufacturer, GM included, was three-row happy at the time and shoe-horning third rows into *lots* of crossover models, even if they were difficult to access or get comfortable in.

Reality caught up with this early set of requirements, especially in relation to crash regulations and passenger safety. The third row necessarily made LAV longer and heavier than a two-row vehicle in order to provide the minimum crash-related clearance for its third-row occupants. The seating itself wasn't anything an average adult or two could easily get to, and it was not suitable for anything but a *very* short trip. Visually, the LAV receded to a stand-up rear end, giving the vehicle a rather blockish appearance. (Figure 14)

As the safety-compliant LAV made its way to focus groups, it received a decidedly indifferent reaction—not even a small group of "gotta have" respondents like CTS would enjoy it. GM's internal forecasting crew went negative on LAV sales volumes, calling it a wagon, which was *not* a compliment. They defended their low numbers by also noting it was a Cadillac.

Geesh!

Art & Science was all about changing that. Chalk that up as just one more part of GM that didn't get the memo.

Focus group feedback did prompt discussion about removing the third row, shortening and lightening the vehicle as a result, and giving design the latitude it needed for the sleeker, fast-back look they had originally envisioned. But the momentum behind "Three Rows for All" was nearly as strong as it was for "Common," and the LAV/SRX was greenlighted for production as it was. It was a competent vehicle to drive, added luster to Cadillac showrooms, and did decent business, but it was not what many thought the third row would drive. No doubt the longer, heavier vehicle, with pleasing but not dramatic styling, held the first generation SRX back.

But Cadillac fought its way into the crossover game, despite lots of doubts in the forecasting trenches. The second generation SRX ditched the third row and became quite a looker—and has been Cadillac's best-selling vehicle ever since.

Dead Duck(s)

Fast forward to July 2002. Bob Lutz, who had been hired the year before to head up product development, said he wanted the merlettes *back* in the Cadillac wreath and crest.

One had to respect Lutz, not just for his position but for his experience with customers, brands, and styling at Ford, BMW, and Chrysler. He was also fond of saying he was often wrong but never in doubt and that he also liked a good argument. He got one from me on the Cadillac wreath and crest.

I told him about the work we had done on the logo back in 1999. Lutz was generally skeptical of research, deferring to his instincts and highly-practiced gut. Still, to his credit, he thought about it some more and soon after sent me a hand-drawn illustration of a bird laying on the ground, beak up, motionless, as if bagged during hunting season.

Like the red duck, the merlettes would *remain* retired.

The foregoing bits of friendly fire certainly made the execution of Cadillac's Art & Science strategy interesting. Anyone would wish for an easier time of it and would have had one if they had more control of the resources needed to do so. That was my experience at Allison Transmission. GM had once been a collection of Allisons with big, fully equipped car divisions leading the charge, but it had evolved into a large, function-region matrix where the car divisions…clearly, the business units closest to customers…no longer had a seat at the table. Like it or not, every brand seeking to succeed had to run through a pretty punishing gauntlet of other agendas, very few having the customer front and center.

And that was just to *agree on* strategy. Holding it together and orchestrating its execution was equally difficult. Huge amounts of energy were consumed overcoming internal resistance, and one has to conclude that, had most of that energy been directed outward to consumers, to competitors, to emerging technologies, GM would have been better off.

In this environment, Cadillac (and GM) experienced some costly losses, but the most important part of Art & Science and its first true market test, the CTS, was still ahead of us and would tell us everything. If it didn't work, Cadillac was a goner.

CHAPTER 7

C(OURAGEOUS)TS

W ayne Cherry's brief from the Strategy Board in February 1998 was unambiguous—show us an Art & Science-imbued Catera replacement in ninety days. In doing so, Cherry would violate all of his own rules, gathering together the best designers no matter which brand studio they were then assigned to. He handed off his administrative duties to his direct reports and poured himself into the effort. Everything would take a backseat to developing a Cadillac destined to challenge the likes of the BMW 3 Series and Mercedes C-Class.

Deploying "Art" to CTS

Cadillac's new form vocabulary was stimulating creativity

among the designers and, overnight, the Cadillac brand character studio became the hottest place to work at Design. More than fifty different interpretations of Cadillac's new design language were splashed all over the walls, studied, and debated—some were discarded, more study and debate followed, and still more sketches were discarded. Eye-catching elements from the various designs, including those discarded, were retained and carried along, influencing the remaining proposals, even stimulating new contenders.

In a short while, Cherry and team were down to a handful of sketches, a small enough number where quarter-scale clay models could be quickly prepared. This would be the first 3D moment, where what appeared to be well proportioned in a drawing could be seen in real life, albeit pint-sized.

A winner would emerge from this second phase, and with

some modifications then incorporated into a full-size 3D model. A lot of math goes into developing a *full-size* clay model of a vehicle (not actually all clay but gobs of it applied to a wood/Styrofoam skeleton). Only after the clay has been roughed in by numerically-controlled machines can the vehicle's life-size proportions truly be revealed and appreciated—or not. In every case, it is quite literally the hand of the clay sculptors, artists all, who render the final surface and proportions, and they do so lovingly, square inch by square inch.

So it was with CTS, a very different animal from every Cadillac in recent memory. Angular, faceted, dramatic—all by design.

Showtime 2.0

By late March, not quite sixty days after the Strategy Board meeting, Cherry's team had completed the clay model in

Cadillac's studio. Design had worked with a very short timeline; so did engineering and manufacturing folks who were working alongside, picking up needed details for budget and capital expenditure estimates. This was the usual parallel pathing that takes place in product development, but CTS would be more involved since it included a new, rear-wheel-drive architecture, multiple body styles and models over time, and a new assembly plant.

While no formal review of the clay was held by the Strategy Board at this time, various board members no doubt took a look during their visits to Design for other reviews. The grapevine was buzzing and in a good way. But Cherry had something else, something better, planned for the formal review of the CTS by the Strategy Board scheduled for the following month.

In early May, the board reconvened in the Cadillac studio to review and hopefully approve the CTS model. Cherry used some of the same long, rolling whiteboards from the dome presentation in February to remind the group about Art & Science and Cadillac's new design language. He then brought down the studio lights and rolled the whiteboards away, revealing the CTS model—this time in gleaming fiberglass, with see-thru windows and front and rear lamps ablaze! (Figure 15)

It was a glorious reveal...met with a stunning silence....

But followed by spontaneous and sustained applause.

To that point in my GM career, I had never witnessed such a response from GM leadership, and I had been involved in plenty of design reveals over the years. Usually, there would be smiles and laudatory comments, but applause? It was pure emotion and great to see. Such excitement, hopefully, would translate into a damn-the-torpedoes effort back in the respective functional silos.

Engineering

CTS was approved for production that day, and the different functions—design, engineering, manufacturing, and purchasing—got a whole lot busier. After design, the most telling work, as far as the vehicle's success was concerned, was done by engineering in developing the new rear-wheel-drive architecture. While GM had converted nearly all of its passenger cars from rear wheel drive to front wheel drive in the early '80s, as a result of new fuel economy rules Congress enacted in 1979, it retained pockets of expertise both in Europe (Opel) and in the US (notably, the uber-talented Corvette crew).

Jim Taylor became the vehicle line executive for the Sigma architecture-based products and, years later, one of my successors as general manager of Cadillac. Taylor asked me to join him in a kick-off meeting at GM's desert-proving ground with the CTS development crew. They had cobbled together a couple of rudimentary vehicles, suit-ably called "mules" in auto parlance, that they would put through their initial paces appropriate for the Entry Lux segment and do so while also driving the leading compet-itive makes.

The development crew was led by Ken Morris, noted for his drive (no pun intended), his competitive spirit, and his highly-calibrated "butt"—the latter a key characteristic of accomplished development engineers. They were excit-ed about their mission and didn't need much motivation from me, although I recall noting this was the chance to put Cadillac back in the forefront of luxury consumers' minds.

Over the next few years, Ken and team, and the GM engi-neering factory, worked the mules into shape, creating the usual long list of parts and their specifications. Such parts are first made as one-offs or in low volume and find their

way into a sequence of prototype vehicles. These prototypes, unlike the mules, look like the CTS, but the prototype process is all about seeing if the parts work together,
both functionally and in form. Many changes and refinements occur in the prototype process, ultimately leading
to the best possible product on the showroom floor.

And it's important to note that a *lot* of CTS's development
work took place on the demanding Nürburgring in Germany. That is where the very best come to test and develop their vehicles, and it contributed greatly to CTS's great
ride and handling experience. As Barry Winfield of *Car
and Driver* observed, having experienced the CTS on this
track before it was launched several months later:

> *The result is a Cadillac like no other, with a ride that is
> firm but not abrupt and one that resists pitch and roll
> without neck-snapping stiffness. As a bonus, the car has
> steering that is linear and readable at any speed. It's all*

in the tuning, and the Nürburgring experience influenced pedal positions, brake operation, and even seat design in this new CTS.

Discriminating retail buyers would appreciate all of this soon enough, but it would also spawn an architecture capable of supporting killer cars on the road-racing circuit and the first-generation V-Series editions some buff books preferred over the established Mercedes AMG and BMW M-Series models.

Journalistas 3.0

In August of 1999, Cadillac hosted our select group of journalists again at the Pebble Beach Concours. This time, however, we showed them production-intent hardware, the forthcoming new CTS, in person and full size. It would, of course, be an off-the-record reveal with no press kits or photos. The full Cadillac team was there, along with the designers Wayne Cherry had chosen to develop the CTS exterior and interior. Ron Zarrella also came along, which would later prove to be so important.

Wayne Cherry began the presentation by reminding the gathering of the ground we had covered together already—the first gathering at the Collection, explaining Art & Science the prior year, Evoq's debut, returning to Le Mans, etc. Evoq was on the small stage, next to Wayne and undraped, leaning into the crowd like a crouched panther. It was the marker Cadillac had put down related to the future design of all its models.

When Cherry removed the drape over the see-thru fiber-glass model presented to the Strategy Board in May, another moment of silence ensued.

Followed by spontaneous and sustained applause.

It had such a familiar and welcome ring.

Pure emotion, and this time from a group of journalists who see *lots* of new products and who might be expected to be a bit guarded, if not jaded, in their responses. This was the kind of reaction Cadillac used to get and was playing for again.

The car was every bit as aggressive and fresh as Evoq, but in sedan mode. Cadillac was staying the course, staying on that journey the journalists had been invited to join early on. I sensed some ownership of the CTS by everyone in the tent. Perhaps the simple act of being honest about the brand's state in 1997, of being transparent as to what needed to change, and asking for thoughts engendered that feeling of ownership, which certainly couldn't hurt when the CTS actually launched.

Jerry Flint, Unbound

Jerry Flint, an experienced automotive journalist, was

with us that day. He had participated in most of Cadillac's select media gatherings. A unique personality in his field, he was not one to mince words. While his vocabulary tended toward "salty," he had seen and driven *lots* of cars and trucks in his career and had heard lots of nice words from various factory types that often didn't ring true to him or were never fully delivered. His subsequent critique of such fluff could be withering.

Flint loved the CTS reveal at Pebble Beach and also loved how Cadillac was changing. A few months later, he was in Detroit having dinner with Ron Zarrella. At some point, the conversation turned to CTS. Flint's enthusiasm for the car was undiminished and said,

> *You know what that car says? It says, 'Fuck you. I'm from Detroit!'*

Zarrella shared Flint's reaction with me the next day, and Ron was clearly excited! It was music to my ears. Flint was voting for a Cadillac returning to its roots of unique and daring styling, celebrating America's can-do spirit—designs once again filled with *attitude!*

Focus Groups...and the Courage of Ron's Convictions

In January 2000, I became general manager of GM's service parts operations division. Service Parts might seem to be an odd next job, but it was (and remains) a key part of any dealer's business, as 40 to 50 percent of gross profits are derived from parts and service. It was a fun place to work and was valuable experience for me when I later became VSSM's group vice president.

While at Service Parts, I received a call from Ron, who by then was president of GM's North American operations. The CTS had recently been shown to focus groups as part of the usual market research done in advance of a vehicle's launch. Such research informs sales volume estimates, advertising, final pricing, etc.

At least, it's supposed to "inform" and be considered with all other data and beliefs the company holds. Research is a tricky business, and there is considerable art, if you will, in its structuring—how the properties are presented, how the questions are raised, how any focus group discussions are processed, who is behind the curtain listening—and drawing conclusions from the discussions, etc. There is also the small matter of handicapping responses for something new and not in the respondents' shared experiences.

Ron talked me through the results. He said there was concern that CTS was not the top choice, although a meaningful percentage chose the car and, in doing so, offered comments conveying a *lot* of emotion. As the CTS was decidedly very new and different, I believed the overall response to be very good and was quite encouraged by the comments. There was a group with which CTS struck a

passionate chord, not unlike that prompting the spontaneous applause from Strategy Board members and journalists when they first saw the car.

And don't forget Jerry Flint's comment!

I think Ron really believed in CTS, and the call seemed
to fortify him. In the run-up to CTS's launch in the fall of
2002, he became like Henry Fonda's character in *Twelve
Angry Men*, repulsing never-ending internal handwring-
ing about the focus group results. Some even suggested
launching the car as a Seville replacement, and at a much
higher price.

This would have been a catastrophic mistake. To his lasting credit, Ron held his ground, providing solid air-cover
to the Cadillac team to launch CTS as the intended Catera
replacement. Then led by Mark LaNeve, Cadillac would
introduce the bold and edgy CTS to the world with inspired marketing, including Led Zeppelin's *first ever* com-

mercial partnership, a fantastic Times Square display, and prominent product placement in *Matrix Reloaded.*

Passion, Patience, Persistence Rewarded

CTS was a *big* success!

Introduced in early 2002 (as a 2003 model), CTS sold nearly 38,000 units that year, growing to nearly 53,000 units in the full twelve-months of 2003 and contributing to a 20 percent increase in total Cadillac sales compared to 2001. CTS sales volumes would steadily increase through 2005, reaching nearly 67,000 units that year.

Forbes' "In the Driver's Seat" review in December 2001 seemed to predict the car's reception in the market:

> *The 2003 CTS...is the answer to the question many of us found ourselves asking whenever we drove particularly satisfying European sedans. This is an Audi, Mercedes,*

BMW type of car that is more than capable of satisfying the needs and desires of that customer base. Once people start seeing the car on the street, we daresay it will generate a following.

From the get-go, Cadillac and the GM Design Staff truly believed we were onto something with Art & Science, and the first *real* market test of this strategy, CTS, proved us right.

CHAPTER 8

REVIVAL!

n the run-up to CTS's launch in early 2002, Cadillac had already introduced some of its good looks with the Imaj concept car and had also introduced the second-generation Escalade in both short- and long-wheelbase versions. Cadillac's return to racing was announced, along with Night Vision on the Deville. The brand was busy and getting more than its fair share of media coverage and luxury-consumer mindshare!

The CTS launch took that awareness up several notches since entry luxury was the largest segment in the US luxury vehicle market and also the most underserved by Cadillac. Over the next few years, Cadillac kept fanning the flames of Art & Science with additional concept cars, including Simon Cox's super-slick, mid-engine Cien on the occasion of Cadillac's one-hundredth anniversary in 2002 and the majestic 1000-horsepower Sixteen in 2003.

2002-2005 New Models

More importantly, from the CTS launch through 2005, Cadillac introduced at least one new model *every year*, a dream scenario for any automobile brand. In 2002, along with CTS, Cadillac expanded Escalade offerings with a long wheelbase model and the addition of EXT (a luxury pickup truck featuring a fold-down bulkhead behind the second row of seats). In 2003, Cadillac introduced the XLR luxury roadster, followed by the SRX crossover and the CTS-V high-performance models in 2004.

This first CTS-V was a head turner, as unexpected and important as Escalade, but fully leveraging the inherent ride and handling capabilities, at the extreme, that a RWD platform will allow. What a rush, and those great GM engineers and racing jocks who created this incredible car had to love what Jeff Koch from Hemmings Muscle Machines had to say about the car:

We have made little effort to hide our mad lust for the Cadillac CTS-V. That week we spent with one a year ago not only provided the most memorable driving experience we've had in a while, but it told us that, after decades of wondering what the hell was going on back at The Tubes (aka GM's Renaissance Center complex), someone at GM actually got it.

Motor Trend observed that the CTS-V *"...could hang with the BMW M5 and M-B E55 AMG, and at a 30 percent lower price!"* (Figure 16)

Cadillac's showrooms were rocking, and the new offerings based on the Sigma rear-wheel-drive architecture were living up to expectations!

Not a One-Hit Wonder

In 2005, the STS premium luxury sedan was introduced, replacing the Seville. This vehicle was especially important in dispelling concerns that CTS (like the '92 Seville) would be just an exception to Cadillac's otherwise big and floaty sedan hardware. (Figure 17)

Ahead of its introduction in 2005, the crew at *Car and Driver* seemed to like it, as stated in an article appropriately titled, "The Kindly Old Barber of Seville Trades Scissors for a Switchblade." Steve Spence said,

> *Here, finally, is something I thought I'd never see: a Cadillac that wants to get into the ring with the big cars from BMW and Mercedes.*

Others chimed in, with Barry Winfield saying:

> *Damn, this STS unwinds a chunk of California's coastline like no Cadillac ever has*

and Csaba Csere stating flatly:

STS is unquestionably the best Cadillac I've ever driven.

With the steady drumbeat of new and critically-acclaimed models, Cadillac's annual sales increased accordingly, from a little over 173,000 units in 1996 (a thirty-two-year low, not counting the strike year 1970) to nearly 250,000 units by 2005. And while not Cadillac's top-selling model until 2005, CTS, along with Escalade, was working wonders in lowering the average age of Cadillac buyers and increasing the percentage of college grads driving Cadillacs.

Hope Delivered

The early work on new retail facility standards enabled a significant makeover of many Cadillac dealer showrooms in line with Art & Science standards, some completed ahead of the CTS launch. Traffic increased and Cadillac dealers parlayed the increase in interest into the sale of the

new CTS, or some other model, or both. Customer satisfaction improved, with Cadillac placing in the top five
of all brands. Importantly, Cadillac dealer attitudes improved—a lot—from among the worst of all automobile
franchises in early 1997 to the upper third by 2005. The
value of Cadillac franchises skyrocketed.

2006 and Beyond

Post 2005, Cadillac continued to bring new stuff to market. V-Series editions of the STS and XLR debuted in 2006,
both sporting supercharged Northstar engines producing
440 and 469 horsepower, respectively. The venerable Deville also got a makeover in 2006 and was recast as the DTS.
While the DTS offered some design changes consistent
with Art & Science, they were limited because the legacy
front-wheel-drive architecture could only bend so much.
The DTS did not last long in the new world.

It mattered not a whit as design and engineering crews at GM did some truly great work on the second and third generation CTS models. (Figure 18) The second-generation CTS was a lovely new sedan that included wagon and coupe models, with *all* getting V-Series treatments shortly after launch. This car won *Motor Trend* Car of the Year when introduced in 2008, and *again* in 2014 when the third generation CTS made its debut.

From the get-go, CTS received high marks from the buff books and consumers. But the continued improvements over subsequent generations received as much if not more praise. The *LA Times*, serving an area *not* known for their love affair with American car brands, noted,

> *Since its inception, the CTS has been a pivotal model for Cadillac, helping to lead a turnaround at the brand after years of turning out dated land yachts.*

Taking the Foot Off the Gas

With Art & Science, Cadillac got back to its roots of making uniquely styled and great driving cars. It also got into the nascent but growing luxury SUV/crossover market with Escalade and SRX. Ditching the unusable third row in the SRX allowed the second-generation vehicle to slim down and have much better styling, selling *twice* as many units in its first year as the three-row SRX did in its best year. (Figure 19)

The third generation SRX was introduced in 2017, and the model name was changed to XT5. With this vehicle also being built and sold in China, XT5 became Cadillac's highest-volume model that year, selling over 145,000 units worldwide.

Despite the success of SRX/XT5, Cadillac was slow to react to changing luxury market tastes and expanding its crossover portfolio, and it paid a price in US sales and market share. Unit sales in 2019 had fallen to a little over 175,000 units—not very far off from the last low point of 173,000 in 1996 before the Art & Science journey began.

In 2018, Cadillac added a smaller XT4 crossover to its portfolio, followed in 2019 by a larger XT6. Hopefully, these new models will reverse the brand's home-market fortunes.

China to the Rescue

Were it not for China, Cadillac's faltering performance in the US might have prompted renewed questions about the brand's staying power. Beginning in 2013, Cadillac's sales volumes began a steady rise in China, helping global sales in 2014 surpass the last high mark in 2005. In 2017, Cadillac sold more vehicles in China than in the US and, because of China, that same year it sold the most cars *in its history*—and did so again in 2018, and again in 2019.

China became the largest vehicle market in the world in 2009, its market having been more or less nonexistent when I first visited the country in 1986. It will *always* be the largest vehicle market and the largest single market for luxury vehicles...for Mercedes, for BMW, for Audi, and for everyone, including Cadillac.

Cadillac's success in China and the explosive growth in sales volume over the past twenty years is a good thing. GM has a lot of mouths to feed, but it also has limits in terms of what the engineering factory and capital expenditure budgets can accommodate at any given time. As in almost every business, decision makers are attracted to where the money is and increasing consumer acceptance as key reasons for continued investment in any brand's new models and technology.

That said, Cadillac's partners in China are, well, the Chinese. It is a fifty-fifty joint venture with one of the very best Chinese companies, SAIC. They are entitled to, and hold, their own views as to what makes for an attractive Cadillac-branded product, and it cannot be assumed they embrace dramatic styling to the same degree we did at the outset of our Art & Science journey. Bear in mind "dramatic" and "daring" overtly traded on American technological prowess and culture, for that is Cadillac's pedigree. It was, then, also a clear source of separation from the other luxury marques, given as they were at the time to more conservative styling.

Having once paid a steep price for playing it safe with exterior styling, for "sanding off the edges" if you will, hopefully Cadillac and its partners in China will hold a shared view of the brand's positioning and the important role that leading-edge technology *and* styling plays in the brand's value proposition. With many Cadillac models now being sold in both the US and China, one can imagine a kind of tug of war between the two markets on styling going forward. If so, hopefully Cadillac's aggressive styling pedigree will not be a casualty.

Cadillac and Alternate Propulsion

As noted previously, in the late 1990s, we believed Cadillac should be the lead GM brand for alternative propulsion technology. Luxury vehicle customers were usually first in line for such offerings and had the means to pay for them. During GM's first 100 years, advanced technology often made its debut in Cadillac models and, over time, found its way into other GM brands. So it should be with alternative propulsion.

In the mid-2000s, hybrid technology became feasible, and by 2009, a hybrid 'Slade was available. It had a battery pack recharged by regenerative braking and a new, two-mode continuously variable transmission. It provided some improvement in fuel economy, notably in the city, but not everyone was crazy about the drivability of the vehicle, nor the option price. It enjoyed a relatively brief run.

By 2006, GM was deep into developing the Chevy Volt. A breakthrough had occurred in batteries, specifically the advent of lithium-ion batteries, offering a number of advantages compared to lead acid (which is what GM's EV1 necessarily had to use). The Volt would package enough batteries to support forty miles on a single charge, noteworthy since the majority of vehicles on America's roads never do forty miles in a day getting to and from work, running errands, etc. Should someone need to go beyond forty miles, a small, range-extending gasoline motor would be onboard—think generator—to recharge the battery.

Volt was a technology development moon-shot and a market test for GM, not so much a source of profit. Considering the knowledge GM obtained, and the positive press, it was good value. It also closed a perception gap with Toyota, who had benefited greatly (some would also say disproportionately) from Prius—a series hybrid featuring a battery pack allowing one to drive maybe ten miles on electric before switching to gasoline power.

Volt would be better. And it should have been a Cadillac, where its audience had both more interest and more money.

In time, GM made a Cadillac "Volt" called the ELR. (Figure 20) It was a beautifully styled car, but otherwise shared everything else with Volt—the same powertrain, same performance, same range...for $75,000, or $35,000 more than Volt! Most of us believed ELR would be viewed as a high-tech Cimmaron by the media. It was also expensive to do, with capital expenditures and engineering expenses in the several hundreds of millions. "Old GM" leadership decided not to proceed.

After bankruptcy, "New GM" leadership greenlighted ELR when it somehow emerged from the dustbin. As expected, the $35,000 premium over the Chevy Volt for different styling and not much more was the stuff late-night comics relish. Only 3,000 units were built over three years, at times with dealer inventory at times calculated in *years' supply*, not months or weeks. Given the low sales and the discounts required to clear the market, the ELR was every bit the lousy investment that "Old" GM knew it would be.

The good news is that GM has now put Cadillac in the lead of GM's alternative propulsion efforts. GM Chair and CEO Mary Barra remarked in January 2019 that Cadillac would become GM's lead electric vehicle brand and become all-electric by 2030, beginning with the Cadillac Lyriq to be introduced in late 2021. Her wingman in this endeavor is Mark Reuss, now GM's president, who noted that he is less interested in answering questions about the "future of Cadillac" than he is in delivering the "Cadillac of (automotive) futures."

Downright lyrical—or is it Lyriq(al)?

CHAPTER 9

IN THE REARVIEW MIRROR

Times have changed in the last twenty years, as have the possibilities, if not imperatives, in the personal mobility market. When conceived, Art & Science served both Cadillac and GM well. For all the difficulties in fighting for Cadillac's first SUV, repositioning the brand, and staying the course, GM's best brand was rescued from the precipice and made significant contributions to the company's coffers. And in its survival, and revival, it gave GM a lucrative chip to play in securing a solid position in the world's largest automotive market, China.

Two big plays stand out in my time at Cadillac—Escalade, for sure, and Art & Science. 'Slade created important new buzz around Cadillac, led to ginormous profits over time for both dealers and GM, and set the stage for other SUV and crossover models to follow that would have Cadillac selling more such vehicles than passenger cars from 2012 on! Without 'Slade, I'm not sure Cadillac would be around today since it arrested the brand's decline.

Art & Science enabled growth, as it defined the look, feel, and technologies of a new Cadillac but one totally respectful of its long history of dramatic styling and industry firsts. The supporting product portfolio played out from 2002 to 2005, with CTS, XLR, STS, an Escalade sport utility derivative, and the first V-Series model. By 2005, Cadillac's sales had risen to a fifteen-year high, attracting more college grads and younger, wealthier buyers.

Sadly, in the years to follow, Cadillac fell on hard times and its home-market sales (the US) have never returned to 2005 levels. The brand no doubt suffered, as did all GM brands, from the effects of bankruptcy in 2009. Cadillac also fell behind in the breadth of its crossover offerings, which other luxury competitors acted on sooner. This has been addressed in the past year or so with the addition of two new crossovers flanking the high-volume XT5. Time will tell if that's the tonic or not.

I believe some part of the brand's decline in its home market can be explained by leadership, more specifically, leadership *changes*. In the twenty-some years since I left Cadillac in early 2000, Cadillac has had *twelve* different leaders, some with different titles but all with the same responsibility. Suffice it to say that such turnover is unusual by any standard, not great for continuity of purpose, and probably not helpful to the top or bottom lines.

As I have reflected on the turnaround at Cadillac from 1997 to 2005, a few observations come to mind that explain the success we had:

- We had an *experienced and talented team* at Cadillac,

with little turnover during the conception and subsequent execution of *all* facets of Art & Science—products, advertising, promotions, communications, etc. We had all-stars at every position, and most of the team later went on to bigger roles, both inside and outside of GM after their time at Cadillac.

- We regarded the work as a *team sport*, and various quarters of GM's far-flung enterprise pitched in. Here, Wayne Cherry and the Design Staff deserve special mention. They are talented, creative folks, and more given to divining the future in a car company than any other function. Wayne reorganized design to work with the brands in a more focused way than ever before, but unfortunately, had too few takers. Bad for them but good for Cadillac, as we got more than our fair share of attention as a result.

- The team also *included Cadillac dealers.* Beginning

with the first conversation I had with Carl Sewell, the dean of all Cadillac dealers, they were on the frontline and knew our customers and other luxury brand customers since the best Cadillac dealers also held those franchises. They were a huge store of valuable information and, given the changes we needed to make in the retail environment, they had to be onboard all along the way.

- The team also *included the journalists.* They see and drive so many products and were good counselors as we were making the Art & Science "sausage." I don't think any of them ever gave up their objectivity when reviewing any of Cadillac's new models, but I suspect it was to our advantage nonetheless to have involved them early in our deliberations.

- Importantly, Art & Science was a *clear, compelling, and concise vision* for Cadillac and allowed many folks throughout the big and functionally-organized General Motors mothership to do their good works. It brought the motorsports professionals to the table with ideas about Le Mans and Sports Car Club of America racing as a means to convey the new message. It inspired engineering to develop the "killer app" in the luxury SUV market, and ever-better rear-wheel-drive models, winning two successive Car of the Year trophies for CTS among many other honors.

Leading change from the middle of a very large company certainly had its challenges, the big ones documented previously in this book. In retrospect, it can be said that the Cadillac team, although discouraged at times, remained resolute that we were pursuing the right strategy. Passion, patience, and persistence were employed at all times, and we never took the first "no" at face value! I will also say that leading from the middle was possible only with occasional *out-of-process interventions*, like Jack Smith's fateful call to me in August 1997, reaching three levels down and inviting my thoughts about a Cadillac truck. Chalk that one up to leaders who manage by walking around, one way or another.

It was a privilege to lead Cadillac at perhaps the most difficult time in its history. It was a storied brand and represented the very best that GM could be. A lot of sports metaphors come to mind like taking the last-second shot that wins the title game or being at the plate, bases loaded, two outs, bottom of the ninth, behind by three runs, and parking a fastball deep over the center field wall. That said, it is a moment to be shared with the rest of the team, the coaches, etc., since they all had a hand in it, one way or another.

Escalade pulled Cadillac back from the brink, and Art & Science breathed new life into an ailing and iconic American brand. As a result, Cadillac enjoyed a kind of revival through 2005. While sales volumes have grown thanks to Chinese consumers, momentum has been lost in Cadillac's home market, the US, proving there really is no end to the process of keeping Cadillac or any other consumer brand relevant and compelling.

But Cadillac is special. It's the very best that GM can be, and it casts a long shadow over every other product that GM makes and sells. It's an everyday report card on the true capability of the GM team. For my money, there is no shortage of passion, skill, and resource for GM to draw from to demonstrate that Cadillac is, *once again,* the Standard of the World.

About the Author

John Smith, a native of Kansas City, Missouri, enjoyed a forty-two-year career with General Motors, beginning in 1968 when he began work at the Chevrolet-Kansas City assembly plant. For someone just a few days removed from high school graduation, the rigors of life on the line in an automobile assembly plant—even if only for the summer—provided John with important grounding for everything that followed.

After receiving a Bachelor's in Industrial Engineering from General Motors Institute (now Kettering University) and an MBA from Harvard, John joined GM's New York Treasurer's Office. This group provided key staff support to the company's top leaders and the Board of Directors, and offered John a top-down view of General Motors' breadth and depth.

Over the following years, John would lead GM's joint vehicle programs with its Asian partners, help establish GM operations in Central Europe after the fall of the Berlin Wall, and be part of the team that developed options for the company's all-important operations in China. Prior to coming to Cadillac, John was posted to Allison Transmission following the collapse of a possible sale of those operations to German car parts maker ZF. John and team developed and executed a turnaround plan for Allison that led to a twenty-fold increase in its sale price a decade later.

John retired from General Motors in 2010 and has since served in a number of public- and private-company roles as company director. He and his wife Nancy are also involved in ongoing relief and social services work in Haiti through Jeremie Rising, a Michigan-based 501(c)(3) non-profit organization.